A Parent's Guide to
Coping with
Autism

D0743770

A Parent's Guide to
Coping with
Autism

Sarah Ziegel

ROBERT HALE

First published in 2016 by
Robert Hale, an imprint of
The Crowood Press Ltd,
Ramsbury, Marlborough
Wiltshire SN8 2HR

www. crowood.com

www.halebooks.com

British Library Cataloguing-in-Publication Data
A catalogue record for this book is available from the British
Library.

ISBN 978 0 7198 1940 7

Typeset by Catherine Williams, Knebworth

Printed and bound in Great Britain by
CPI Group (UK) Ltd, Croydon

DEDICATION

For Thomas, Benjamin, Hector and Marcus

CONTENTS

PREFACE

I HAD BEEN A nurse and was now a mother of twins, but I had never met a child with autism until the day a doctor declared out of the blue that both my boys, then aged nearly three, had autism and that there was little I could do about it. He was wrong. There is much that a parent can do, and I have spent years acquiring that knowledge.

At the time of the diagnosis I desperately wanted a book to read that would give me hope and tell me what to do. I could not find one. Thirteen years later, I now have four beautiful boys – all with autism – and a world of hard-learned advice to pass on, so now I have written that book for you.

Autism is a complex, poorly understood disability, and as parents we are often isolated and left to fight our own battles. We fight for what our children need and deserve and if it seems there is little empathy for our children, there is often even less for us as parents. So this book covers not only the practicalities of how to help your child, but also the emotional impact that having a child with autism inevitably has on a family.

Most importantly perhaps, I wanted to convey a message of hope. My boys were all diagnosed with the more severe form of autism at an early age, but each one has developed and changed into a wonderful young person who has exceeded all our expectations. Their success is all the proof we need as parents to persevere and never give up hope.

I hope this book will help you on your journey, whether you are a parent or someone who would like to understand more about coping with autism.

LIST OF ABBREVIATIONS

ABA	Applied Behavioural Analysis
ADD	Attention Deficit Disorder
ADHD	Attention Deficit Activity Disorder
ASD	Autistic Spectrum Disorder
BAS	British Ability Scores
CBT	Cognitive Behavioural Therapy
CHAT	Checklist for Autism in Toddlers
DCD	Developmental Coordination Disorder
DLA	Disability Living Allowance
DSM	Diagnostic and Statistical Manual
DWP	Department for Work and Pensions
EEG	Electroencephalogram
EHCP	Education and Health Care Plan
ENT	Ear, Nose and Throat surgeon
EP	Educational Psychologist
GP	General Practitioner
IEP	Individual Education Plan
IQ	Intelligence Quotient
LA	Local Authority
LSA	Learning Support Assistant
NAS	National Autistic Society
NHS	National Health Service
NICE	National Institute for Health and Care Excellence
NT	Neurotypical
OCD	Obsessive Compulsive Disorder
OT	Occupational Therapist
PDD-NOS	Pervasive developmental disorder – not otherwise specified
PECS	Picture Exchange System
SENCO	Special Educational Needs Coordinator
SEN	Special Educational Needs
SEND	Special Educational Needs and Disability
SLT	Speech and Language Therapist

1

GETTING A DIAGNOSIS

ONE OF THE CRUELLEST twists in the diagnosis that is 'autism' is that nearly all children with autism will be born without any obvious disability (the exceptions being a child born with Down's syndrome or another coexisting condition). When your baby is born, you will have absolutely no idea that he or she is anything but perfect. If you have a child with Down's syndrome, you may be aware of this pre-delivery or from birth, but you will have no indication that your child too may additionally develop or show signs of autism in a few years' time. But first, what is autism?

A History of Autism
The diagnosis of autism was first defined by Leo Kanner in 1943. He used the word 'autism' from the Greek *auto* (meaning 'self') to describe children with certain symptoms that meant they seemed to live within themselves. His definition of autism requires that symptoms are apparent by the age of three and is also known as *classic autism*.

The other two most well-known disorders in the autistic spectrum are *Asperger's syndrome*, which is a milder form of autism in which there are no delays in language but there are significant problems with social communication, and *pervasive developmental disorder – not otherwise specified (PDD-NOS)*, which may be diagnosed when the full set of symptoms or criteria for autism or Asperger's syndrome are not met.

Very sadly, in the 1960s, Bruno Bettleheim, the director of

a home for disturbed children, had a theory that autism was caused by cold and emotionally distant mothers whom he called 'refrigerator mothers'. Bettleheim felt that these mothers were to blame for their children's development of autism. At the time this was thought to be an acceptable theory. So, for an earlier generation of families with children with autism, there was little or no help or support available and, in addition, the mothers were blamed for their children's problems. To us now, this seems inconceivably cruel and quite medieval in basis. Although his theory has been totally disproved, even now you may sometimes hear mention of it and some parents unfortunately may still feel, or be made to feel, that they are in some way to blame for their child's autism. People may ask indirectly whether you suffered from post-natal depression or something which they may feel led to you not bonding sufficiently with your child. There is another disorder – if that is the right term for these conditions – whereby a child may be diagnosed as having an attachment disorder. This is a disorder that usually affects children who have been adopted or placed in foster care at a very early age and, although some of the symptoms may be similar to those presented by a child with autism, it is indeed a very different disorder with a totally different cause.

Did I Cause My Child's Autism?
Do not let anyone try to tell you that in some way you have caused your child to have autism. Because it is thought that there is a strong genetic link, some grandparents do not wish to be implicated in any way and will try to 'blame' their child's partner for any problems the grandchild may have. You may hear comments such as:

'Maybe it's because you were on the pill for a while, dear, before you had children.'

'Perhaps it's because you are a vegetarian.'

There is no substance to any of these comments as a reason why your child has autism. The thought of an inherited link is one which grandparents often do not wish to acknowledge or accept, so they may try to pin their own theories onto you. Do not take it to heart, but do not accept blame, either. *You* have done nothing wrong.

Would you get the blame if your child had diabetes or was deaf? In the same way, why should parents (very often the mothers) get the blame – if there is, indeed, any blame to apportion – for their child having autism?

Acceptance of your child's diagnosis is one of the very hardest things. Some people never really come to terms with it, but the more you are able to accept it, the better you will be equipped to deal with it and to help your child. And the first stage in this acceptance is that it is not your fault that your child has autism. 'Four children with autism? You must have done something very bad in a past life' – and this from a lady I did not even know! You will have dark days when you will allow yourself to wonder what you might have done wrong, but actually you will have done nothing wrong, so try to banish this negative thought if it pops up. Once you accept that you are absolutely not to blame for your child's condition, you will also be better equipped emotionally to deal with anyone else who comes along trying to apportion blame to you, the parent. Try not to have regrets about what you may or may not have done during pregnancy or in the first few months after your child's birth. It will not help you and it will not help your child. There are too many mothers of children with autism who still feel in some way to blame for their child's condition, so it is important to keep emphasizing this point. This unnecessary guilt will consume you and add to any other regrets you may be holding onto, and will not help you or your child.

Why Does Any Child Have or Develop Autism?

Autism appears to affect children from a wide range of circumstances with no common denominator to predict its arrival. You may have conceived your baby naturally or via assisted conception (such as IVF); you may have given birth naturally or by an assisted delivery (such as a Caesarean section) – however your baby was conceived or delivered, you now have a baby with autism.

Two of my boys were delivered naturally (albeit with a lot of additional help being twins and one of them being a breech delivery) and two were delivered via Caesarean - but all four have autism.

Your baby may have been born early or late according to the due

13

date you were given and be a single child or perhaps one of twins. All sorts of theories exist about possible early signs of disability, such as a child being in the breech position (bottom or feet down) pre-delivery, but most breech babies are totally unaffected by any learning disability. *Two of my boys were breech – one being the second twin – and two were head down (cephalic delivery), but all four have autism.* There are so many variables involved in trying to determine what may or may not cause or indicate autism and many, many theories put up by parents and by professionals.

The chances are that at no time during your pregnancy will anything have been found to indicate any risk of your child developing autism. Your baby will have developed normally in the womb, nothing untoward will be detected on any scans or pre-natal tests, and at birth, any possible complications at birth will be the same, statistically, as for any newborn child.

Your little boy or girl will be cherished by you and loved from birth. He or she will probably start to achieve all the usual early milestones within the normal timescales as other babies, some earlier than average and some later.

Of my four boys, one walked independently at ten months (which is quite early) while another of my boys seemed to 'cruise' for ever and wasn't walking independently until twenty-two months (which is quite late). Both were just within normal limits, however, and gave no indication of anything relevant, although since then both have turned out to have hypermobility (where the joints are over-flexible).

What I am trying to convey is that the diagnosis of autism will come as a huge and devastating shock to you, as to nearly all parents. Maybe there will be a gradual realization that something is not quite right, but having looked after and loved your precious child for a few years, with no inkling of what is to come, the diagnosis will hit very hard. Overnight it seems as though your normal, healthy child has changed into a child with a lifelong disability seemingly from nowhere and for no reason. Suddenly you have no idea what the future holds for you and your child. One day they are fine, and the next they are not.

Some mothers have noted later, looking back sometime after diagnosis, that perhaps their babies were more unsettled than others and were not good sleepers. Such babies may have cried more than some, but other babies too may be unsettled for many reasons and not then go on to develop autism. They may have developed a severe colic, which causes a tiny baby to be very unhappy, yet still there is nothing to really alert you to the fact that something serious might be happening to your child. If you are a first-time mother, you will have no real comparison of your own. Even so, all babies are different and some are easier than others, no matter what you do. So, at the time, you may think your baby is a 'difficult' baby – and, actually, they probably are – but at the time, you may not know any different. Everyone's view of what is difficult to cope with is very subjective and people's tolerance of difficulty also differs greatly, so unless you are a very experienced carer of babies, you may not have realized at the time that your baby is perhaps more unsettled than most.

My twins were my first-born babies. Looking back, they were incredibly unsettled and I hardly ever got any sleep, but I was so proud to have had twins that I struggled through. I thought that this was just how twins were.

Can Autism be Prevented or Cured?

There is some ongoing research, which is hoping to be able to detect and predict early symptoms in young babies that might warn of the condition earlier. Much of this research is being carried out on the younger siblings of children affected by autism. But currently, there is nothing known absolutely to prevent the development of autism. However, it is agreed that an earlier diagnosis is very much more beneficial for the child as it means you can begin therapies and treatments at the youngest age possible to give your child the very best possible start in life.

The Wide Spectrum of Autism

The hardest part is that no one really knows yet why or how a child develops autism. Are they born with a genetic predisposition to developing autism? Is there one trigger or many triggers and, if so, what are these? There also seem to be many types of autism within the same diagnosis: no one child is exactly the same as another and none has the same symptoms; unlike, for instance, deafness, which can be measured as the level of decibels a child can hear, or visionary problems, which can also be similarly identified and measured. Because of the huge differences in the way in which a child may be affected, the condition is defined as Autistic Spectrum Disorder (ASD), which covers a wide range of ability and disability. This also makes any future prognosis difficult, e.g. predicting how well your child will progress and what you can hope for in the future. The definition of ASD is a very open and seemingly vague one in some ways. It means that children diagnosed on the Autistic Spectrum can be affected at very different levels, ranging from the profoundly autistic child who may not ever develop language or be able to live independently to those children at the higher functioning end of the spectrum, usually labelled as having Asperger's syndrome. Again, this makes the diagnosis hard to pin down for parents.

When you first hear the term 'autism' used about your child, what do you think of? Perhaps the stereotype of an autistic savant such as the character portrayed by Dustin Hoffman in *Rainman*? Perhaps you may have read popular novels featuring children with Asperger's syndrome? Perhaps you may already know a child with autism and may think 'but *my* child is not like *that* child'? Of course, we parents are people, too, and inevitably we will jump to conclusions and, sadly, will often assume the worst-case scenario that we can think of. Conversely, you may know someone whose child was thought to have autism but actually the diagnosis turned out to be wrong, so you will hold onto the thought that it also may not be true of your child.

The consultant who told me that my twins had autism also told a neighbour the very same week that her son had autism. Three children in the same road in the same week? It turned out that her son was bilingual and that was the only reason for his language delay, so I clung to the hope that perhaps the consultant had also got it wrong with my boys and that maybe they had something like verbal dyspraxia (*see* page 69). I spent the next few weeks while we waited for a second opinion trying to convince myself that my beautiful boys had any number of issues, but not autism.

Your reaction may also depend enormously on how the diagnosis is delivered to you. If you have a sensitive paediatrician or other professional, you may at least come away with some hope and ideas and positive thoughts about where to go from here. If your diagnosis is given to you by someone with negative thoughts about autism, you may come back from your consultation devastated and with no proper advice for the future of your child.

The consultant told me that my twins were autistic out of the blue during a hearing test, not a developmental assessment, and compared the condition to vegetable soup saying that 'if we all had a bowl of vegetable soup, some of us would have more carrots in theirs than others'. He then sent me away saying there was nothing I could do about it and he would see us again in six months!

Comparing such a serious diagnosis to a bowl of soup is fairly unbelievable and to offer no advice or hope in such circumstances is appalling. However, as a parent there is much you *can* do about it, and it did not take me long to discover that.

Early Signs and Symptoms in Developmental Milestones
The very earliest symptoms of autism may be noticed in a child by experts or by someone with some prior knowledge of the condition from around the age of twenty-four months. Usually it is not very apparent until between eighteen months and two years of age that there may be something developmentally delayed or different about your child. Little things like a child not waving 'bye, bye' may be put down to the child being shy or just late in developing. A typically developing child may put up their arms to you to signal that they want to be picked up and use many other non-verbal gestures like these before they start to talk. These little gestures will occur naturally and you will not necessarily be looking for them, they just happen. You probably will not even be aware of these gestures as you will just respond accordingly to your child if they indicate non-verbally that they need something.

Pointing
If your child does not use physical prompts to communicate with you, you will probably not notice their absence or even be aware that they should be doing some of these things. If lots of these little gestures are missing, this may add up to a bigger picture overall, but each on its own may go unnoticed or not be seen as being significant.

17

One quite significant example of non-verbal communication is the act of pointing. A child should start to point at objects that they want or need or maybe just to draw your attention to something they have seen. Perhaps they will point at a dog or a car or something that catches their interest to show it and share it with you – this is called *joint attention* and is one of the first things a child should begin to do, even before they develop speech. They will point repeatedly at an object that they desire that is out of their reach in order to gain your attention so that you can get it for them. So, pointing with an index finger is an early, very important skill. But again, if your child is your first-born child, then you will not necessarily know what to expect them to be able to do and at what age.

Obvious milestones like rolling over, sitting, crawling and walking are all significant stages of development that everyone readily discusses. Indeed, the age at which a child first 'performs' each of these milestones is often a source of pride to the parents, particularly if they think that their child has achieved it earlier than others. In fact, there is not much significance at what age a child reaches a milestone as long as it falls within the quite wide age range for each activity. Less obvious developmental markers such as pointing and waving are not discussed with quite such enthusiasm and may even be performed by a child for a while before the parent actively notices.

At developmental checks, you are asked at what age your child first sat independently or walked unaided. Most parents have a clear memory of when this was and can pinpoint an exact age. When you are asked at what age your child first babbled or pointed, you may be quite vague or unsure about when or if your child babbled at all.

Usually, parents will remember their child's first word, if they are lucky enough to hear it. For most parents, that word will just come naturally, seemingly effortlessly. For those of us with children with autism, that first word will be hard won and longed for and all the sweeter when it is finally heard. One of my boys' first words was 'juice' (or at least an attempt at that). Hearing the words 'Mummy' or 'Daddy' are a lot further down the line than for typically developing children whose first words usually include a version of 'mama' and 'dada'.

Avoiding Eye Contact

If you are asked when your child first began to point at things, you may suddenly realize that they may never have pointed at all but, until you were asked, you had not noticed or realized the significance of this. Appropriate eye contact is another function that may be impaired but which you may also have not noticed. A shy child may try to avoid direct eye contact. You may perhaps think your child is so absorbed in other activities that they do not have the time to look up or look at you. Eye contact is quite difficult to quantify or describe and some people are naturally better at it than others. A child with autism may appear to be avoiding eye contact deliberately. But, again, until this is pointed out to you, you may not have noticed it at all.

Speech Delay

Of course, speech is the most obvious red flag that there may be a problem. Speech develops at different ages: often girls speak more fluently than boys at a younger age and first-born children also tend to speak earlier. Youngest children in a large family may not feel the need to use language until quite late as their siblings may be doing all the talking and interpretation for them. In twins, language can be delayed or be acquired in a slightly different way. Children who are brought up bilingual can also begin to talk markedly later than their peers. Thus, there are many variables influencing the age at which a child begins to speak. Despite this, there are ages by which certain targets of language attainment should have been reached. One of the more obvious signs that a child may have more than a straightforward language delay is that not only do they not speak, but they also appear not to understand.

You may first become concerned that perhaps your child cannot hear properly. Perhaps they do not seem to respond to their name when called or when talked about. Typically developing children will often turn when they hear their name spoken, even indirectly, in conversation. They will certainly respond when being called or talked to directly and their name used as a command to gain their attention. A child with autism might respond to their name, but not nearly as often as you would expect. Strangely, a favoured word like 'chocolate' may bring a better response than simply calling your child's name!

It was only when I asked my boys if they would like some chocolate and got no response that I realized that not only did my boys not speak, but they also did not understand language. When I produced a packet of chocolate and showed it to them, their response was, of course, immediate and they became very animated and, clearly, they did want the chocolate.

You may have to put yourself right in front of your child to gain their attention – not because they cannot hear you, but in order to try to get any response from them at all. You may also find it hard to make eye contact with your child and may need to put your face within their range of vision instead of expecting them to look to you.

Often, delayed language is not picked up on until you start to become concerned that all the other children the same age as your child are starting to talk and your child is not. Your child may be strangely silent, or not make much noise at all; they may never have made much sound vocally, or at least nothing resembling the beginnings of speech. They may have babbled as babies, but not developed speech following on from the babbling. Or they may have begun to babble and then seem to have lost the babbling somewhere along the way.

One of my twins made a loud continual humming noise from around the age of two which he didn't lose for years until he finally replaced it with speech. It wasn't a form of communication, just a sound that seemed to comfort him or that perhaps he just enjoyed hearing.

Even harder for a parent in some ways is when a child has begun to talk and has the beginnings of speech but then slowly loses all their words and seems to slip into autism. This can happen quite gradually over a period of months until you realize that something is wrong or can happen almost overnight. This pattern occurs in the regressive form of autism and sadly is not uncommon.

Could Speech Delay be due to Problems with Hearing?
So, your child is not talking yet and, to get to the bottom of this, you embark on a round of hearing tests and doctor's appointments. It is quite difficult to test a young child's hearing accurately as not only do they need to be able to cooperate with the testing procedure, but

they also need to understand what is being asked of them. At the same time, they need to be willing to take part and be able to pay attention for the duration of the tests. Not easy at all. Most babies will have had their hearing tested at birth so you should already know that your child is not profoundly deaf. However, it will be hard to ascertain if they have an actual hearing problem.

Sadly, a hearing problem can often be nothing more than a big red herring at this stage. All four of my boys were diagnosed with glue ear, which took months and months of testing to prove, and then further months for treatment to be carried out in the form of the surgical insertion of grommets. Grommets will not be put in until it can be proven that your child has had a minimum of six months of glue ear – by which stage you have been following the path of hearing loss for nearly a year. You are, quite naturally, under the illusion that once the hearing issues have been rectified your child will then begin to speak. If your child continues not to talk post-operatively or post-treatment, then you start to realize that the hearing issue may not be the only problem your child has – and realize that you have been in effect been delayed by another year before the possibility of autism is suggested.

How Long Will a Diagnosis Take?

The diagnosis of autism can take a very, very long time, yet it is in your child's best interests to have a diagnosis as early as possible. There is no instant blood test or brain scan that can be carried out to confirm the condition. As yet, there is no genetic test available, although research is underway to try to prove genetic links and predisposition. You may start with taking your child for hearing tests and to see ear, nose and throat surgeons (ENTs), and then progress to seeing speech and language therapists (SLTs), educational psychologists (EPs) and paediatricians. Maybe your health visitor or nursery teacher will be the first person to pick up that your child is having some problems even before you see any of these experts. Each professional may do his or her own observations first, and it may take a while before you are referred to different specialists. All of these referrals and assessments can mean that the road to diagnosis can be a long one. Within the NHS there are, of course, waiting lists and sometimes long delays before you even manage to get an appointment with some specialists.

Identifying the Early Signs of Autism

There is a checklist for autism in toddlers, known as CHAT, which was developed to help identify children who might be at risk of developing social communication disorders. CHAT is usually used at around eighteen months of age, or whenever there is any cause for concern. It is often carried out by health visitors or nursery staff and is intended to highlight children who might need further evaluation. It is not used to diagnose autism, but is a simple way of assessing which children need some follow-up and even perhaps a referral. If there are concerns on testing, the test should be repeated a second time a month or so later, after which the child should be referred to a specialist, often the community paediatrician. At this you will be asked questions about your child. For example:

- What are your child's play skills?
- Does your child point with an index finger?
- What early communication sounds or words has your child used?

There will also be observation questions for the person doing the assessment. It is quite a straightforward test to carry out and is basically a tick list. If there are concerns following this basic assessment, then a proper referral should be made as soon as possible.

Criteria for Diagnosing Autism

Diagnosis these days is based on some pioneering research by Lorna Wing and Judith Gould in 1979 and is the basis for the triad of impairments upon which the diagnosis of autism is currently made. For a diagnosis to be made, your child must exhibit one or more symptoms from each of three categories. There is a wide variation in the symptoms that each child exhibits and no child will have exactly the same symptoms as another. The severity of the symptoms also varies enormously across children on the autistic spectrum. Your child may have a severe impairment in one area and only be mildly affected in another, e.g. a child with Asperger's will usually have normal language development but may suffer from anxiety or have significant problems with social interaction.

The three categories for the diagnosis of autism are:

- social impairment
- social communication and language impairment
- rigidity of thought, behaviour or play known as social understanding.

If you want to read the official list of criteria used by the medical profession, look up the diagnostic criteria for autistic disorder in the *Diagnostic and Statistical Manual of Mental Disorders, Fourth Edition* (DSM IV), published by the American Psychiatric Association (APA).

Social Impairment

Social impairment can include not responding when being talked to, as illustrated by behaviour such as:

- not turning or answering when their own name is called (even though you know they can hear you)
- seeming to be in a world of their own for a great deal of the time, which may result in the child playing alone and not being aware perhaps of other children playing around and alongside them
- appearing not to notice the presence of other people, which might result in the child actually bumping into other people or not moving out of the way as you would expect them to
- pulling you by the hand for you to reach the desired object for them, but without any eye contact or pointing to the object
- very little or poor eye contact, even to the extent that they may actively dislike being made to look someone in the eye and find it quite uncomfortable to do so
- a marked dislike of physical contact such as cuddling, which can be very distressing if a child falls over and needs physically comforting but rejects you and cries alone.

One of the most strongly held beliefs that seems to prevail is that all children with autism show no affection and actively dislike physical contact. It will often be one of the first questions someone may ask you on hearing that your child has autism: does your child dislike physical contact? In fact, many children with autism are more affectionate than others who don't have it, as children with autism act instinctively without worrying about what other people may think of them.

Social Communication and Language Impairment

Social communication and language impairment can vary greatly in severity. Some children may have no spoken language at all and may appear not to understand any words either. The levels of spoken (expressive) and understood (receptive) language are usually fairly equal in a child with autism. This means that a child with only a few spoken words probably only understands a few words spoken to them unlike, for example, a child who may be selectively mute and may not speak but who understands what is being spoken to them. Babies start to learn language and will cooperate and do things on command before they start to speak, which shows an understanding of language (receptively) before they begin to actually say words, e.g. asking them to clap their hands or get their shoes. A child with autism may have no understanding of language and therefore have no idea of what it is you are asking them to do, but if you physically do the action in front of them, e.g. you clap while you saying 'clap hands', then your child may cooperate and perform the same action. Your child will have understood by observing and repeating what they have seen you *doing*, not by understanding what you have *said*. Children learn naturally by imitation, but a child with autism may not pay sufficient attention and observation to others and therefore often will not imitate.

Echolalia

Often without any real understanding of what is being said, your child may repeat words spoken to them: this is known as *echolalia*. If you ask a simple question, they may repeat whatever you say straight back to you. Thus the question 'Do you want juice?' comes straight back at you as 'Do you want juice?', but if your child has some language ability this can then become complicated by them getting the pronouns mixed up. So, when your child wants some juice and asks you for it, what they may actually say may be 'You want juice', as this is what they have heard said to them as opposed to realizing that the pronoun 'You' should change to make 'I want

24

juice'. If you ask your child directly whether they want juice, the correct response would usually be 'Yes', but you could still have the words repeated back to you – and, in fact, they may not even want any juice at all! A child may repeat the last word or two of everything you say with no real understanding and, when offered a choice, will usually appear to take the second option as they are repeating the last word they heard. For example, if you ask 'Do you want a biscuit or a piece of cake?', they may say 'cake' while grabbing the biscuit from you. In this way, language is acquired and used in a very different way by children with autism. Children with no communication difficulties will acquire language almost effortlessly whereas a child with autism finds it very difficult and will often need specialist teaching and intervention to be able to communicate at any level. Speech in a child with autism can also take the form of narrating chunks of language learned from favourite books or films, often known as 'scripting'. To an outsider this can sound as if your child has language ability but, in fact, this is not an effective form of communication. Your child may not even understand the words they are repeating, but they may like the sound the words make or perhaps the words make your child happy because they are thinking about that favourite part of a film or book. Your child may also talk nonsense jargon, which they think is speech as perhaps speech sounds like nonsense to them.

Does a Lack of Language Mean Low Intelligence?
It is important to emphasize that although your child may not understand language, this does not mean that they have low intelligence. Sadly, many people assume that lacking language does indicate low intelligence.

If you were to move to China tomorrow, would you be able to work/answer the phone/watch a film or read a book in Chinese, whether Mandarin or Cantonese? I know I wouldn't. I would find it hard to learn much more than my own name. Certainly, I would not be able to function in life in the way I do in the UK. This does not make me unintelligent; it just means I can't understand the language. It does not diminish from my own understanding of the world, or the intentions and purpose I may have. This is the closest I can come to explaining how my boys function and feel in our world without the communication skills they so badly need.

Non-Verbal Children

At the time of diagnosis some children may have no spoken language at all, only sounds that they make and, as such, are termed non-verbal. It is hard to predict at a young age how much language a child may go on to develop as they grow older. Most children do acquire some form of communication eventually, but in more severely affected children, language may be largely substituted for other forms of communication such as sign language/PECs (Picture Exchange Communication System) or even keyboard skills. There are also children who can speak but who do not see the point of talking for talk's sake. Such children may speak when really necessary, i.e. when asked a direct question that requires an answer, but otherwise they do not feel the need to initiate a conversation.

I spent years desperately wishing that my boys would talk and now that they can, I sometimes find myself wishing they could just stop talking for a few minutes, which seems so ironic. Although my boys have grasped the use of speech, they have yet to learn the social skills in using speech, e.g. waiting until the other person has finished speaking in order to speak or realizing that if all four of them begin talking at the same time, this means that I can't actually listen to each one and reply all at once!

Some children may speak in a monotone voice, or too loudly or too quietly. They may have strange intonation or pronunciation. They often have their own agenda, which could mean talking endlessly on their 'chosen' subject, which may be an obsession with, say, trains or characters from a cartoon. You may try to start a conversation with your child, who may then go off on a totally different tangent that leads back to their chosen topic. Conversation should be a two-way process and, ideally, it should engage both parties having that conversation. A child with autism may appear almost to be having a conversation with themselves.

Rigidity of Thought, Behaviour or Play Known as Social Understanding

Children with autism often display rigidity in their play and thought. Your child may be obsessed with playing with their toy car or train. This is often because they enjoy spinning the wheels or pushing the car (or train) back and forth repetitively. The way in which your child plays with the actual toy may therefore be very rigid as your child may not acknowledge the purpose of the car, i.e. to transport people. The spinning of wheels or watching the train go back and forth over and over again may absorb your child for hours at a time. You may see them lie on the floor and get very close to the object so they are at eye-level with it. This behaviour can be known as 'stimming' or self-stimulatory behaviour. The point is that the toy is not used for its intended purpose as a play object or to represent something real in miniature. Some children line up cars or similar small toys in rows and may wish everything to be in a certain order. Your child may carry around an abstract item, like a piece of string, from which they will not be parted even though this item is not a toy or comforter.

When he was about two years old, one of my boys carried around a broken toothbrush holder. It served absolutely no purpose and he didn't play with it, but he would not let it go. It was his comfort blanket for days.

A toy may be used as an abstract object, so a child might use a small doll to bang in a nail or dip a car into their yoghurt and eat from it. Although some children play appropriately with their toys, it is very common for a child with autism to lack these appropriate play skills.

Some children like to sniff or smell everything. They obviously have a strong sense of smell and this can put them off eating certain foods. They may also refuse to eat something because of its appearance. (Little children can be fussy eaters at the best of times, so you may find your child eating a very limited diet for many reasons.) Your child may also venture up to a stranger and sniff them, which can be very hard to explain. *I tried to disguise some fish oil (a good source of Omega 3) by hiding it in mini muffins. After this, one of my sons took to sniffing everything suspiciously before he would eat it! Can't say I blame him, though, as fish oil can have a pretty disgusting smell.*

Rigidity in routine can create huge problems for you as a parent. Your child may insist on a very exacting routine that must be the same every time; if not carried out in the same way each time, this could cause the child great trauma, which may often result in a tantrum. For example, your child may insist on walking a certain route to a familiar destination, e.g. the local playground, and if you try to vary the route your child will refuse to walk and may lose their temper. Similarly, your child may always want to sit in the same place. This may be fine at the family dinner table, but can create problems if your child insists on sitting in the same seat on a bus where someone else is already sat. Your child may have no flexibility in the order in which they do anything and so everyday processes become part of a ritualized and rigid routine, which must be maintained if your child is not to become distressed.

The Long Journey to Diagnosis

Getting an actual diagnosis from a professional can be a very long process. Some local authorities seem reluctant to diagnose.

To a cynical parent like me, this may be because you as a parent may try to get some help from the local authority, which it is obliged to pay for. So, the longer your child remains undiagnosed, the less money the local authority will have to spend on he or she. Like the NHS, the local authorities (LAs) have spending limits, and it does seem in some areas that getting a diagnosis for a child takes longer and is a lot harder to obtain than it should be. Meanwhile, time is ticking away for your child: the earlier you can start therapy and get the appropriate help, the better chance your child has in succeeding in the future.

Private or NHS Diagnosis?

If you are fortunate, you could be referred to a multi-disciplinary team, which may consist of a psychiatrist / speech and language therapist / clinical psychologist / educational psychologist and paediatrician, or a combination of some of these health professionals. In many areas, you may see the community paediatrician only, but you need to be sure that the person giving a diagnosis to your child is a health professional with experience in diagnosing ASD.

Even after my community paediatrician announced out of the blue at a hearing test that both of my twins had probable autism, all I finally received after that visit was an appointment for a formal diagnosis to be carried out in a year's time by the NHS. As far as the community paediatrician was concerned, there was nothing I could do about my boys' diagnosis so there was obviously no need for speed! So, of course, I had no option but to seek a private diagnosis as I wasn't prepared to leave my boys without help for another year.

If you do decide to get a private diagnosis, again be sure that the professional you consult is recognized as an expert in the area of ASD. Meanwhile, be sure to remain on the NHS waiting list as you will still need a formal diagnosis from the NHS in order to access any services being offered. Your private diagnosis may be acknowledged by your LA, but often the LA will not offer services for your child until it has carried out its own formal assessment. Your private diagnosis will get things moving quicker, as once you have a formal diagnosis you can get started with helping your child.

Some private medical insurance companies may be willing to pay for an initial consultation that may lead to a diagnosis and a full report if autism is not a named condition on your policy. You may need to see other specialists to rule out any other conditions, such as epilepsy, or problems with hearing. Private medical insurance does not cover chronic disease and so conditions like autism are not covered. Once your insurer has paid for an initial diagnosis, it is very unlikely to pay for any resulting therapy required by your child.

Private health cover may be willing to pay for some speech and language therapy if your child has needed surgery for grommets for glue ear, for instance, so it is worth asking. If you do not have private cover, then do check first how much a possible diagnosis and report will cost you. It may be relatively expensive, but these will strengthen your child's case as no one will listen to you until you have a diagnosis from someone, somewhere, to prove that your child does have autism and needs help. If you know that you will have a long wait for your child to be properly diagnosed, then a private diagnosis may be money well spent, if only to get the ball rolling and perhaps speed up other services.

In an ideal world, your child would be seen and diagnosed as soon as a problem becomes obvious but, in reality, the LAs and the NHS like to play a game of 'let's wait and see' in many cases.

The Sub-Categories of Autism: High-Functioning/Low-Functioning

We have seen that there are three main 'types' of autism – Asperger's syndrome, PDD-NOS, and classic autism (page 11). This last category also often gets further divided into sub-categories. Your child may be labelled 'verbal', i.e. he or she is able to talk, or 'non-verbal', which means that he or she is not making any vocalizations that resemble speech, although few children are truly silent. Your child may also be termed as 'high-functioning' or 'low-functioning', which can be quite controversial labels. High-functioning implies a more able child with perhaps a higher IQ and better language, whereas low-functioning implies a more severely affected child who is less able to cope in mainstream life. Early on, it is often difficult to place a child in any category at all, and really trying to define where on the autistic spectrum your child appears to be is not really the point. With the right support and help, your child, who may have been non-verbal and seemingly low-functioning at diagnosis at a young age, may then progress to using functional language and begin to understand the world in which they are a part of. At this point, they may be deemed as being high-functioning.

IQ testing

There are many issues around the accuracy of testing a young child's intelligence quotient (IQ) level when they have very little language, and so, perhaps with some justification, these sub-divisions are not very accurate. IQ tests are not devised for non-verbal children, and so a child with very little language can often receive a low score as they will score badly in the sections requiring language. Your child may be very able in one area while being much less able in another.

As my two boys could not follow instructions or questions, at diagnosis they were considered non-verbal and supposedly low-functioning. But now they are certainly deemed to be high-functioning as they have a wide vocabulary and can function fairly independently.

If you say that your child has high-functioning autism, people may assume that your child has Asperger's syndrome. In fact, there is a big difference between high-functioning autism and Asperger's.

Asperger's syndrome is used to describe children who have an IQ of over 70 and who have had little or no delay in acquiring language. It is not, therefore, possible to change a diagnosis from autism to Asperger's later on, even if your child improves hugely. Why? It is because you cannot remove the fact that your child had a delay in acquiring language. In this case, your child's label should remain as high-functioning autism.

Try to remember, though, that these labels and diagnoses are solely meant to enable you to get help and support for your child. The label is not necessarily the most essential element, but authorities do require some sort of label in order to be able to place your child and help with their needs – and it is your child's individual special needs that are what is most important. Just stating that your child has autism is not enough. Your child should not only be labelled as a child with autism, but also as a child with perhaps severe speech and language delay or with behavioural problems or whatever it is that your child has problems with. Whatever problems your child has, therefore, these need to be addressed and appropriate support given. These needs could encompass language, behaviours, academics or social problems, but could also include many other issues. It is important that people do not only look at your child as having a label – or, even worse, as *being* that label – but as an individual with individual needs. Later on, your child may acquire additional diagnoses, such as attention deficit activity disorder (ADHD) or dyspraxia, which also come under the umbrella of ASD. Some children may also have medical diagnoses not covered by the ASD diagnosis, such as epilepsy.

How Early Can a Child be Diagnosed?
You may have noticed something about your child that has caused you concern and prompted you to ask for some advice in the first instance. Perhaps you have noticed a lack of speech or rigid patterns of behaviour.

I did not notice anything particularly different about my twins when they were little: they were my first-born and I just thought that twins were very hard work. I was also told that they were speech-delayed simply due to them being twins, so I did not see the need to request a referral for my boys to any professional.

Particularly with a first-born child, you may not be aware of anything being wrong or different about your child until perhaps they start to go to nursery and mix more with other children of a similar age. At this point, you or someone else observing your child may begin to make comparisons and notice that your child is possibly delayed or different in some way from other children. Ideally, the referral process and road to diagnosis will be started as early as possible in order for the support to be put in place to ensure that your child gets the best possible chance to do as well as they can.

Again, I cannot stress enough the importance of an early diagnosis so you can begin to help your child as young as possible. It makes me very sad when I meet parents whose children did not start to access help and therapy for many years. Those early years are crucial for our children's development.

Some of the Professionals Involved in Diagnosis

There are a number of different professionals who may be involved in making the diagnosis for your child. You may already be in touch with a health visitor, or you may be advised to set up a meeting with a heath visitor in the first instance. A health visitor is a qualified registered nurse, midwife or sick children's nurse, or even a psychiatric nurse with a specialist qualification in community health. The health visitor is part of the NHS and they are often closely linked to general practitioners' practices. Every family with a child under five years old should have a named health visitor. You will probably have met your health visitor at a baby clinic, which you would have attended with your newborn baby. Apart from regularly having your baby's weight checked, you can consult the health visitor for parenting advice and tips on feeding, weaning, etc. If you are lucky, you will have been offered an eight-month baby check or a two-year-old developmental check. During these checks any potential problems may have been identified, so you may already be in the system and have been referred already to other services. However, as with most non-essential services within the NHS, many health authorities have cut back on the funding for these checks and you may only be referred or be offered a check if you or another professional thinks your child may benefit from an assessment. The health visitor may do a general assessment on your child and talk to you about any concerns you may have, and then may do a CHAT checklist as mentioned earlier (*see* page 22). This is not a definitive test or diagnosis and is designed only to identify children who may possibly have some form of communication disorder and who would benefit from a formal extensive assessment. Some health authorities additionally have a special needs health visitor who you may be able to consult. They will have a greater knowledge of the issues around having a special needs child and can offer advice on facilities and benefits available in your health authority.

Audiometry or Hearing Tests

Your next point of referral may be a speech and language therapist, particularly if your child is not talking. If this is the case, you should also be referred to a community audiologist at the same time, as your child's hearing should be checked first. It can be very hard to test the hearing of a child with ASD as they will have difficulty in responding and cooperating with the testing procedure. Even with expensive equipment, there is no definitive test that can assess your child's hearing levels without the cooperation of your child.

Firstly, your child needs to wear headphones, which may be the first stumbling block if your child refuses to wear the headphones. Ideally, sounds should be transmitted through the earpieces to give a pure sound unmasked by any other background noise. If you child refuses the headphones, an operator can sit behind them with a hand-held machine that emits bleeps at different decibels (or levels of noise). But even if you can get your child to sit still and listen, they then need to be able to press a button or move a toy (or something) to indicate that they have heard each sound. In a sophisticated audiology clinic, there is a silent booth with glass boxes with moving toys inside. These boxes will light up and the toy will move. For example, a toy monkey clapping cymbals to prompt a child to look in the direction of the toy, to see the source of the noise. Even this is not 100 per cent accurate as the child may anticipate a box lighting up and look to the box without waiting to hear the sound. The staff in such centres are often excellent and well used to testing children with ASD, but if your child is unable to sit quietly and do as expected, ultimately the test will be impossible to perform.

Glue Ear

The only test that can be done more easily is *tympanometry*, which measures the vibration of the eardrum (tympanic membrane) and can indicate whether your child has glue ear, which is causing a level of conductive hearing loss. Even this test needs your child to sit still for a few seconds, but they do not have to actively take part, no understanding is needed on their part. If this test does indicate that your child has glue ear, you will be asked to bring them back for a repeat test in two or three months' time.

Glue ear is a build-up of fluid behind the eardrum, which prevents the eardrum from vibrating in response to sound waves. The presence of fluid in the ear has been likened to listening under water, so all noise is blurred and indistinct. There seems to be a higher correlation of glue ear with children with ASD than in the neurotypical population. If your child does have glue ear, this may explain a degree of language delay and perhaps some behavioural problems. A child with glue ear who does not have autism will still have appropriate eye contact and joint attention. That is to say that they will point at items and try to share their ideas with you and will be able to indicate in non-verbal ways that they need something. A child with both autism and glue ear will be doubly disadvantaged in trying to acquire communication skills, both verbal and non-verbal.

All four of my boys had glue ear, three of them requiring operations under general anaesthetic to insert grommets and drain the fluid. Before we could begin to teach them language, they needed the procedure to be able to hear sounds and language in the first place.

If your child requires medical intervention for glue ear, they will then be referred to an ENT surgeon if repeated hearing tests over six months show glue ear and consistent hearing loss. There are other things you can do to try to resolve the fluid without surgical intervention. Removing dairy from your child's diet can reduce the level of mucus produced. You can try cranial osteopathy to extend the canal behind the ear drum in which the fluid is found in order to increase the flow. You can also try more alternative treatments such as hopi candles and homeopathy. Because you have to wait six months for referral for surgery, you have plenty of time to try out some of these therapies without causing any delay in treatment.

I have to admit I tried them all for my youngest son, including hopi candles on alternate days for six months. My osteopath even admitted that my son was the first child whose glue ear he had not been able to resolve and so my son had the grommets inserted. Within one week of the operation my son was able to walk as, previously, the fluid had also been affecting his balance and he had only been able to cruise the furniture until that point. As a result, the surgery made a huge difference to my son both in his ability to walk unaided at last and also to hear sounds properly.

Speech and Language Therapists

Whether or not your child has glue ear, or any other form of hearing loss, you should be referred to a SLT if your child has any signs of language delay or disorder. Speech and language therapists do not only advise on the acquisition of spoken language, but also other forms of communication such as non-verbal communication. These may take the form of a sign language such as Makaton or the usage of PECS (Picture Exchange Communication System).

SLTs also advise on children with eating or drinking difficulties. Some children with ASD have a very restricted diet that is self-regulated. This means that a child refuses to eat certain foods and may only choose to eat a very limited range of food. In some cases, this can mean ingesting only fluids or puréed or soft foods as the child may dislike chewing food because of the texture of certain foods, such as meat.

My boys ate a great variety of home-cooked puréed food happily for three years, but when we tried to introduce food that needed chewing, they refused to eat much of it. Their enlarged tonsils also made it hard for them to swallow effectively.

One of the problems that can result from not eating solid foods is that the muscles around the mouth do not get much exercise (from the chewing action of the jaw) and, consequently, are not worked properly. This will further hinder a child's acquisition of speech and their formation of verbal sounds. If your child is similarly affected, do ask your SLT for help.

An SLT assessment can be part of the process of getting a diagnosis of ASD for your child. The assessment will not be a one-off session, but should be carried out over a period of time so that information can be gathered from parents and other people involved with your child, such as nursery staff. The assessment will include observation of your child's understanding of spoken and body language (known as 'receptive language') and your child's ability to use spoken and body language (known as 'expressive language'). In a child with ASD, the level of receptive and expressive language may be at a very similar level to each other so the child will only understand as many words as they can actually say. The child may be able only to understand and speak certain words, or they may have a slightly higher level of understanding than they can speak. For example, you might be able to ask your child to 'get the ball' and they will comply, but if you ask them to label the ball and ask them 'What is that [i.e. the ball] called?', your child may not be able to reply correctly (by telling you that the object is a ball). Your child may only understand the word 'ball' and not the overall question 'What is it called?'

Some children may have no awareness of language at all and may make little meaningful noise themselves. If a child were deaf and did not have autism, they would respond very differently and be trying to communicate in other ways to convey things to you. Their non-verbal communication would probably be very good and they would be able to interpret body language and have appropriate eye contact. To these children, language is just a jumble of sounds that has no meaning for them.

A child may have a relatively good level of vocabulary, but in a social context they may not use it in a meaningful or appropriate way. Some children talk in a script-like way, repeating learned chunks of phrase. To outsiders, it may appear that the child has highly developed language skills, but it may be that the child is using memorized words that they can form but which they could not expand upon or even use in the correct context.

More able children with good language skills may not respond appropriately to questions and may talk on a theme that interests them regardless of the person they may be talking with. In fact, it may feel like there are two separate conversations going on: one that you are trying to have with a child and a second that the child is having on their own behalf.

An SLT will also observe a child's play skills, e.g. their pretend or imaginative play, assess whether they have the ability to copy play or to join in with an activity. The assessment may take place at home, in your child's nursery, or in a speech and language clinic. Your child may be observed playing with certain toys or being asked questions about those toys. The SLT may observe how your child asks or requests for an item they want, perhaps by asking for the object by name, by pointing at the object or by grabbing or snatching at the object. The SLT will also observe whether they look at you or the person with the object first in order to request it. Many children with autism will not look up to the person with the desired object, but will instead reach or grab the item without any eye contact first.

There are formal speech and language tests that may be carried out, although these will probably not be used on very young children. So, a lot depends on a number of factors: the age your child is when they are going through a period of assessment, pre-diagnosis and the actual standardized tests carried out.

At school age, more formal testing may be carried out and you may be told that your child's language is within a certain age level. Generally, the assessment will look at all the areas around the development of speech: expressive and receptive language; non-verbal communication; play skills; and social skills.

Educational Psychologists

Your child may also be assessed by an EP. If your child is pre-school age, you may be offered a home visit or the EP might visit your child at nursery, if this is appropriate.

If your child is school age, there is usually an EP attached to your child's school, and a referral may be made by your child's school for an assessment. An EP no longer has to have a teaching degree, although many do have this additional qualification. They do have a postgraduate specialist degree in educational psychology, which is undertaken after an initial psychology degree.

The assessment will include observation of your child, as well as a great deal of information from a parent or carer about your child, so that an opinion is made not just on a single observation. Your child may behave very differently on different days or when with unknown people or in new situations and places. It is, therefore, of great importance to have your input and knowledge of how your child behaves. Your child will be observed while playing and some toys may be provided to see how your child plays with them, e.g. to see if your child plays appropriately with small characters (such as putting dolls into a doll's house and then acting out stories with the dolls). Perhaps, instead, your child will use the characters as objects for building with and not treat them as dolls but as inanimate objects. This may indicate whether or not they are not playing with the toys appropriately. A lack of imaginative play and a tendency to play in a limited way is very common in children with autism.

An EP will try to assess your child's cognitive (intelligence) skills at the same time. This may be done with the use of puzzles or tasks using blocks and shapes. It is possible to approximately assess a child's cognitive ability even when they have no understanding of language, although the results may not be totally accurate. The tasks may be done a few times and timed in order to calculate a level of understanding. These may involve copying a task or trying to do something independently, such as completing a puzzle or sorting objects. The EP will also assess your child's verbal and non-verbal communication and use of language. For example, does your child point at objects? How appropriate is their use of language and is it being used in the right context?

Behaviour is a very important indication of ASD as children with autism tend to display some or several of the behaviours associated with this disorder. For example, your child may be very rigid in the way that they go about certain tasks or they may insist you do things in a rigid way too. Your child may have rituals surrounding certain everyday tasks, such as brushing teeth or going to bed. If these rituals are broken and cannot be adhered to, your child may experience meltdown and temper tantrums. Commonly, children may line up objects like toy cars, or order toys into colours rather than playing with them. They may have obsessions with certain things such as water. A child may flap their hands or jump and up down when excited. There are many different behaviours and it is important that you are able to tell the EP all the behaviours that your child exhibits as these may not all be observed during one session or assessment. The EP will also need to know how long your child can concentrate on a task, or even how long they can concentrate when doing something of their own choosing.

Self-help skills are another area of child development that can indicate if your child has a problem. A developmental delay in feeding or dressing oneself may be identified. Some problems such as an inability to do up buttons at an appropriate age may be due to motor issues, which could mean that your child has a level of dyspraxia. A cognitive delay may also cause poor self-help skills.

An older child may be assessed using the British Ability Scores (BAS) tables.

Paediatricians and Developmental Testing

You will also see a paediatrician (children's doctor) who specializes in the area of child neurological development. This visit will be held at a neurodevelopmental clinic. In order to see this type of specialist you will need to be referred by another professional, e.g. your health visitor or GP, who has concerns about your child's development. There may be a long waiting list for these appointments, which can be very frustrating.

The paediatrician will take a family and birth history of your child. They will also ask about any medical problems your child has had in the past or is suffering from now. Your child's developmental history will be asked for, so it is useful if you can jot this down and also take with you to the appointment all the dates and ages at which your child achieved certain milestones (for example, the age at which they first smiled, started to babble, to roll over, to sit up unaided, to crawl, to cruise the furniture, and to walk unaided).

The paediatrician may carry out a Ruth Griffiths Mental Developmental test. This scores a developmental age for certain areas. The areas covered are:

- motor skills, e.g. physical skills such as climbing the stairs or hopping on one foot
- personal and social skills, e.g. self-help skills and eye contact
- language skills, e.g. both verbal and non-verbal.
- eye and hand coordination (assessed by observing your child draw or build towers of bricks)
- performance, which tests cognitive skills such as completing a puzzle.

All these areas are given an age score, which is compared to your child's actual age. Your child may be age-appropriate in some areas and delayed in others; they may even show unusual skill and ability in one area. Finally, your child will be physically examined and have their height, weight and head circumference measured and rated on a centile chart, which compares your child with other children of the same age. If there are any physical characteristics noted, your child may need to have some further tests such as a genetic test for Fragile X (*see* page 67).

You may see all of these professionals or you may be asked to attend a clinic that is multi-disciplinary, which means that more than one specialist may observe your child at the same time in order to be able to discuss their findings. This service should all be provided by your health authority, but you may be referred out of the area if there is a specialist clinic better able to meet you and your child's needs. The process can be lengthy and you may decide at any point to see any of these specialists privately in order to speed up the process and obtain a written and proven diagnosis for your child. If you do this, it is very important to continue to see all the people you are asked to see under the NHS. If you opt out of the initial assessments offered, you may find it very hard to stay in the system and later obtain the relevant services and support, such as speech therapy, that your child may require. You will also need to stay within the educational and health service because at a later stage you may need to seek an Education and Health Care Plan (EHCP) for your child. If you do see both private and state-funded experts, you should inform them at your appointments that you have done so as some tests can only be carried out at certain time intervals, e.g. a test such as the BAS should not be repeated in the space of a year.

How Long Does it Take to for the Assessments to be Completed?
All of this testing and assessment process can be very draining and take a long period of time. You may be desperate to get on and get started with helping your child as the process goes on. Unfortunately, if you are using state-funded services (such as speech and language therapy) there may be a delay in actually getting the help your child needs. You will get to a stage where you just want to know what, if anything, is wrong with your child and

demand some firm answers. The professionals may want to consult further with each other and compare notes on your child before giving you a definite diagnosis. After all, you would not want a lifelong diagnosis applied to your child if it were not true, would you? Having said that, it is rare for a child to be mis-diagnosed with autism. In very able children with Asperger's, the diagnosis may be quite hard to ascertain as other psychological conditions may have to be taken into consideration and ruled out. Your child may have problems socially or have high anxiety levels, but these could also be due to other circumstances or disorders. A child with severely delayed language who has no hearing problems and who has other issues will be more obvious to diagnose. There may also be differential diagnosis in a non-speaking child. For example, a child may be selectively mute, i.e. they are choosing not to speak for some reason, but their level of understanding of language will be very different from that of a child with a form of ASD.

Try to remain positive while all this is going on. Do not look too far into the future, or try to second guess what is wrong with your child. If it seems likely that a diagnosis of autism will be given to your child, then you may want to start to look at what is available in terms of support and education. You can apply for Disability Living Allowance (DLA) pre-diagnosis as this allowance is based on your child's needs and not on a diagnosis. In the same way, you should push to get speech therapy started if your child has language delay and you do not need to wait for a diagnosis for this, either.

Your child may need help at nursery, perhaps in the form of one-to-one assistance and you do not need a formal diagnosis to obtain this type of help. The head of the nursery should be able to apply for this extra help on your child's behalf while you are waiting for a possible diagnosis. You may wish to start the EHCP process at this stage, too.

2

COPING EMOTIONALLY WITH A DIAGNOSIS

How CAN A PARENT possibly deal with the enormity of the fact that their precious son or daughter has been given a diagnosis of autism? How does it affect a grandparent or another child in the same family that their grandchild or sibling has autism?

Initially, a huge wave of different emotions will overwhelm you. Most parents' first reaction will be a state of shock that their perfect baby and child appears to have developed a seriously disabling condition seemingly out of the blue. It can feel almost as if your child must have suffered a head injury or some other form of brain damage, but without the accident or the illness to cause it. How can it possibly be true? Alongside this reaction may be another of disbelief. Maybe the diagnosis is wrong? Maybe you need a second opinion? A severe disability cannot possibly arise without a cause, can it? Your reaction may also be affected by the manner in which you are told the diagnosis and the length of time it has taken to get to the stage of a final diagnosis. However nicely it is worded and however sympathetic the delivery, for most people it is still a devastating diagnosis to receive. Grief is a very natural reaction and all of us will feel the need to grieve in some way when we first hear the word autism. The extent of an individual's grief will be dependent on many factors, not least the severity of the autism in the child who has received the diagnosis.

The Stages of Grief
Elisabeth Kubler-Ross explained the five stages of grief in her 1969

book on *Death and Dying*. Although she was primarily writing about dying, her explanations of grief can be applied to other situations where a great deal of grief is present. The stages progress at different rates according to people's ability to deal with each stage. Some people never reach the end-stage of acceptance.

Denial

The first stage is denial. You may be in this initial stage on hearing the diagnosis for the first time. This may mean that you may not want to believe the diagnosis that your child has been given and think that it may be a mistake. You may seek a second or even third opinion in the hope that your child may have been misdiagnosed and that someone will tell you it is not really true. Some people will take the diagnosis on board straight away, particularly if there have been obvious signs for a while, so you may pass through this stage relatively quickly. Sadly, sometimes parents will not even acknowledge a diagnosis and will not accept it at all. They may not seek out a diagnosis or may even refuse assessments for their child. They may not wish for help for their child as they may believe that things will change and that their child's problems are only temporary. There are also some cultures where autism may be seen as a mental disability, which may not be socially acceptable in that culture. So these parents may remain in denial or may try to keep the diagnosis hidden from others around them, which also means they may not do very much to actively help their child progress. If you do not believe a diagnosis or accept that your child has autism, then you are not very likely to accept that they may need some extra help.

The fact that you are reading this book means that you are not in this category, but you may come across other parents on your path in the future who are stuck in the denial stage. This is a very sad place for both themselves and their child to be. Between parents, too, there can be different levels of denial. A mother may accept that her child has autism but the father may remain in denial of it for a much longer time. Both parents may accept the diagnosis of their child while perhaps the grandparents or other key family members are unable to.

Older generations may also have a different attitude towards disability. Autism or ASD is a relatively new condition and there are still many people who do not have any idea of what this actually means. Someone from an older generation may not be willing to acknowledge that it is a definable, lifelong condition. To them, it may seem to be a label to attach to a child who they perceive perhaps as being naughty and who, with the right parenting and discipline, will be fine in a few years' time. Obviously, if you do not really believe in the condition itself, then how can you believe that a child you know well has it? If families are divided on whether a child even has autism, life can be very, very hard. Hard for those who do accept it and want some help and understanding, and hard for those in denial who are waiting for 'it' to disappear. If one parent wishes to pay for therapy or to send a child to a special school but the other parent does not agree, how does a family hold itself together?

Anger

The second stage is anger. This may result in a feeling of life being totally unfair. Why me? Why my child? Who or what has caused the autism? Who can we blame? Are we to blame? Most importantly of all, parents should in no way blame each other. You created a child together. If it turns out that one of you may possibly have some genetic predisposition to any disease or disability, that does not mean it is that person's fault or, indeed, anyone's fault for carrying that possibility.

Some parents believe that their child's autism has been caused by childhood vaccinations. Their anger is therefore directed against the drug companies who produce and endorse these vaccinations as being safe and necessary. The vaccination debate is a huge issue and highly emotive. Such parents may blame the drug companies or the government, but they may also blame themselves for allowing their child to have the vaccinations in the first place. Anger in this case is directed against a corporate being and not an individual.

Some parents will find dealing with their anger harder than others, depending on their individual situations and emotional makeup.

When my twins were diagnosed with autism, I was very sad and very frightened for their future and ours, but I would not say that I was angry. Perhaps I channelled any possible feelings of anger and went into 'action mode' instead – indeed, I don't think I have ever stopped being in that mode. However, when my third son was diagnosed, I was very angry. I already had two sons with quite severe autism. I certainly felt that I didn't deserve or need another of my children to have the same condition. Although the anger steered me through the whole process yet again, I remained angry for a very long time. Occasionally, when we are going through a rough patch, that anger rears its head again and the questions 'Why me? Why us as a family?' return. But, thankfully, the feelings of extreme anger wear off again as whatever situation is causing it, is resolved.

Anger is an awful emotion to live with on a daily basis. A little helps us to galvanize ourselves into action, but living with permanent anger can be very destructive. It can wreck people's lives so that they cannot even enjoy the things that they should be able to enjoy, destroy relationships and even cause physical problems. Like depression, if feelings of anger are overwhelming and do not dissipate over time, some professional help may be needed, perhaps in the form of counselling. Some people find gentle activities such as yoga or meditation can help them to release anger. Others may need more physical exercise in the form of sports such as running, gym training or swimming to help clear their minds and release stress.

Along with anger about your child's condition, you may also experience anger with those around you. You may be jealous or envious of other people's children who do not have the problems your child has. You may feel other people are boasting about their children's abilities and are not being sympathetic to the problems your own child may have. You may not want to spend time with people who make you feel angry in this way. This feeling may be totally justified (in which case these people are to be avoided). It may, however, be that you feel angry in general at your perception of other people's lives and find it hard to be happy for them. Protecting yourself from potentially difficult social situations may be the best way to deal with your anger until it lessens and you are able to look at other peoples' lives in a calmer way.

It may be hard to contain your anger when people around you make comments about your child when they do not realize that your child has a disability. Many children with autism have no outward signs of being different and so you may be judged solely on their behaviour. There is a great deal of ignorance about autism and how it causes behavioural problems in children. If you are feeling stressed and emotionally fragile, a stranger making a negative comment about your child or your parenting skills may cause you to snap and lose your temper. In time, you will almost certainly have to develop a thick skin where other people are concerned or your anger will consume you. Some parents carry cards briefly outlining their child's condition to hand out to strangers. This avoids confrontation and helps to educate others. If you do lose your temper, a stranger may wonder why you are so 'touchy' as they will have no idea of what you may be going through.

Bargaining
The third stage of grief is bargaining. Depending on your own beliefs, you may wish to bargain with a higher power in the form of prayer in order for your child to be made well again. You may offer up aspects of your own life in return for your child not to have autism. A more positive form of prayer would be to ask for divine help so you are able to look after your child and for your child to be as happy in their life as they can be. But if you are bargaining, it is only natural that you will wish for your child to be free of autism and for something to be taken from you in exchange.

You may be able to turn this bargaining stage into a positive whereby your part of the bargain is to do everything you can to enable your child to fulfil their full potential. This may involve self-sacrifice in the form of not being able to work and so reducing your personal income. At the same time, you will increase your potential spending on your child so you will have to sacrifice further things in order to be able to balance your family finances. The bargaining will be that if you do the best you can for your child, your child will achieve the best in themselves. You may well continue this bargain for the rest of your child's life.

The bargaining may lead you to think that the more you spend on therapy, the better the outcome for your child will be. Sometimes this will be true and sometimes it will not. Bear in mind that it is not always about money, but sometimes about choices and trying to make the right decisions.

Depression
The fourth stage is a hard one: depression. In the case of living

and looking after a child with autism, depression can also be compounded by extreme tiredness. In the early years of coming to terms with a diagnosis of autism, depression is very common. It may take a milder form where you grieve in a normal way, which may mean you cry on a very regular basis. It would be quite strange if you did not grieve at all, so you should be gentle with yourself and let yourself cry when you need to. In the early days, you may cry a lot, possibly daily, but with time this overwhelming sadness *will* lessen. It is important to go through this stage of grieving and not to hold all your grief within yourself. You may need to keep your life confined during this stage. You certainly do not need people trying to cheer you up and telling you that it is alright when to you it is not. Many people cannot cope with another's grief and will try to jolly you out of your sadness or worse, try to change the subject and distract you. It makes them uncomfortable to see you upset and so they wish to change it. You will quickly come to realize who your friends are that can be relied upon and who will be gentle with you when you need it. Often what you most need is a hug and some words of support, not someone telling you that you should be grateful for what you have.

Feelings of extreme sadness and depression should lessen with time. If these feelings do not appear to be lifting at all, or they become worse and prevent you from leading a 'normal' life, then you should seek some professional help. Of course, you may well feel an enormous amount of grief and become depressed in the early days of coming to terms with your child's diagnosis. This level of grief is natural and should be an acute, that is, a short-term state of being. You cannot sustain high levels of severe emotion on a long-term basis. You need to consider your own well-being as well as that of your child; if you are living with depression, you will not be able to help your child, either. Professional help may come in the form of therapies such as formal counselling or cognitive behaviour therapy (CBT). It may even be necessary to seek medical advice from a doctor if you develop clinical depression.

If you have been sleep-deprived for years, perhaps due to your child having problems with sleep, then receiving a diagnosis of autism for your child may help you and others to appreciate why you are feeling so run-down. Sleep-deprivation is certainly responsible for causing many physical and emotional symptoms. If you have sleep-deprivation, coping with life can seem an uphill struggle every day. If you then add a diagnosis of a lifelong disability for your child on top of your state of sleep-deprivation, life may become too much to cope with. Looking after a child with autism is exhausting, adding all the therapies, appointments, paperwork and everything else to your life is utterly exhausting. It is hardly surprising that some people become depressed. Others may actually be treated for depression with medication when perhaps what they really need is sleep. How wonderful it would be if we could be given sleep on a prescription from the NHS!

Acceptance

The final stage of grief is acceptance. By this stage, you should have accepted the fact that your child has a condition known as autism. The doctors or EPs are correct and you can accept that at this moment in time your child definitely has autism. Having said that, I personally do not believe that you have to accept how your child actually is and all the limitations that may be present as being fixed and unchangeable. In the explanation of this final stage when someone is dying, the acceptance stage means they accept the truth of their mortality and that they are going to die. When we apply this to a child's diagnosis of autism, I think it needs to be seen as a basic acceptance of the initial diagnosis. I do not agree that you have to accept everything that goes with it. The fact that many mothers do not accept their child's autism as being final means that they continually fight to change their child's condition. This fight can take many forms: fighting for therapies, for funding or even to get a diagnosis in the first place. There is potentially so much improvement that can be made and no one should be made to feel that all the symptoms of autism displayed by a child at the time of diagnosis are fixed and unchangeable. There are some people who are so acceptant of their child's autism that they do not feel a need to fight so hard and are able to love and appreciate their child for who they are. Sometimes, people will say that they would not change their child and remove the autism even if they could, as it is part of who their child is. For the majority of parents, though, we would do anything to remove the negative aspects of our child's autism. It does not mean that we do not accept or love our children. For me, it is because I love them so much that I wish an easier life for them. So, for those of us fighting to lessen the impact of the autism in our children, perhaps acceptance is never going to be a true state. The removal of some aspects of autism will not change your child's personality, it will allow their true being to be revealed.

Grief is Unique to Each of Us

It is important to remember that all these stages of grief will progress at different rates for every family involved. The extent of the grief and how it manifests itself will be individual to every person affected. Although the parents are usually the most involved, and it is they who carry most responsibility for a child, there are others who can also be greatly affected by the new diagnosis of a child. A young sibling will not be able to comprehend such a diagnosis and will probably carry on as before, accepting their sibling for who they are. An older sibling may be capable of understanding some of the aspects of autism and so may also go through some of the stages of grief alongside their parents. Grandparents may take the news badly as their future hopes for their role as grandparent have been changed radically. In an ideal world, a grandparent will love their grandchild with a disability just as much as they love their grandchildren who are not affected. As we know, though, you can choose your friends, but not your relatives. Sadly, sometimes the people you look to for support are just not there to give it to you. Their feelings consume them and they are unable to see past their own thoughts to be able to empathize with you and yours.

Living Loss

There is also a state described as 'living loss'. The term 'loss' on its own is usually applied to people who have lost a relative through death. The addition of the word 'living' turns the loss into a state of 'living loss', i.e. literally, a state of loss while someone is still alive. It can also be interpreted as a state of living with loss on a daily basis. You may have lost the person you believed your child would be in the way that a serious accident or illness would have changed their life, too. You may grieve daily for the child without autism whom you may have known for a few years and whom you now have lost. In their place, you have been given a child who does have autism. You will have daily reminders of how things might have been and how your child might have progressed had the autism not been present. You may rightly feel that you have lost so many things a parent should look forward to in their child's life. In the early days there may be things you miss acutely, such as your child not calling you 'Mummy' or being totally disinterested in opening their own birthday presents. As time goes on, these things will change; perhaps your child will begin to talk and call you 'Mummy' in an appropriate way. But there will always be a sense of loss, however great or small, for so many situations and different aspects of life.

Initially, you will be much more aware of what you feel your child has lost than your child will be. A child's own awareness of their condition may not be apparent for a very long time. So you will be the one living with that sense of loss, of what might have been. This is something that may remain very present or may come and go depending on other factors. You may feel it acutely when your child is among other children who do not have difficulties and who may be achieving significant milestones such as speech. It is also hard when a child manages to catch up with their peers in one area only to realize that those peers have now moved on to the next stage. So you seem to be always in catch-up mode.

Your sense of loss may also be very dependent in the future on how your child perceives their own world. We all wish for a child to be happy above and beyond almost everything else. If your child grows up to be truly happy and content with their world as they perceive it, then this can go a long way to relieving any feelings of loss we may have on their behalf.

> Now that they are able to cope better in the world, my boys are intrinsically happy with their lives. They are joyful in what they do and bring joy to those around them. We try our hardest to make their lives as happy and fulfilled as we can, which can be hard work for us to maintain sometimes. If they are not aware of their loss as we perceive it, should we be constantly wishing for what cannot be?

So, are we grieving for them and what they have lost, or for ourselves and what we feel we have lost? It is probably a mixture of both. The very worst sense of grief we feel is when a child realizes what they perhaps are unable to do, but wish very much that they could. Then we feel so powerless in being able to fix it for them.

How Will a Child be in the Future?

Another very natural reaction is to jump ahead in time and try to imagine how life will be in the future. You may meet up with parents who have older children with autism or whose children are young adults. Even if their child had similar problems to your child at the same age, this does not necessarily mean that your child will progress at the same rate. There are new therapies being developed all the time and old therapies are being refined so that children diagnosed now should have a much better prognosis than those diagnosed a generation ago. So a comparison of a young child's life with that of an adult living with autism may not be a good or fair comparison. Some children may improve greatly, often due to the determination of their parents, but perhaps also due to the degree of autism they have. Some symptoms may lessen and others increase in the future, so a very young child of perhaps three years old at the time of diagnosis can change dramatically over the course of a few years.

I think when my third son was diagnosed I was so upset because I already had two older boys with autism and, of course, that meant that I had a very real vision of his future in front of me. In fact, although he functioned at a similar level to my two older boys at diagnosis, over time his symptoms have lessened much more than those of his brothers. This is despite the fact that they all went to the same school, did the same therapies and even shared the same one-to-one tutors. So, in my case, looking into the future just made me more miserable.

No one can accurately predict the progress any child will make as they grow up. So little is known about the causes of autism, its actual cause may be different in individual families. If no one can prove exactly how and why it happens, how can they then predict how it will progress? Therefore, try to remain positive and believe that all that you do for your child can make a huge difference to their future. Taking each day as it comes is rather a platitude for us and perhaps implies a little too much acceptance. Rather, stay one step ahead and be planning your child's next achievements. Do not look too far ahead, but far enough to be ready in time for decisions about education, schools and possible therapies.

51

Acknowledging a Diagnosis

Getting a diagnosis for your child will have a huge impact on your life and theirs. This is a lifelong condition that you now need to acknowledge. All your hopes and dreams for your child may be swept away in a single moment. All parents want only the best in life for their children, and autism is definitely not part of that ideal picture. There may have been signs that something was not quite right for a while, but it is human nature to be optimistic and to perhaps hope that whatever is happening to your child will resolve itself soon.

Even health professionals may have been telling you there is nothing to worry about; that your child is just a bit later in achieving their milestones than others. Maybe you have twins so 'of course' speech will be delayed. Perhaps you'll hear other well-meant and reassuring words, which aren't really that reassuring at all. Being a cynic, there seems to sometimes be some reluctance on the part of some health professionals to diagnose a child as it may mean money will need to be spent in support of that child.

Other People's Reaction to My Child's Diagnosis

Probably by the time your child gets a formal diagnosis, you will have had some worries about their development. But that does not mean that the diagnosis will not have come as a huge shock and that you should have expected it all along. It does not mean you have had your head in the sand in denial of your child's problems. It simply means that, like every other parent, you will have hoped that your child will be alright and that nothing too serious is going on. Friends and family may have been trying to reassure you that you are imagining problems and think that you are over-exaggerating about your child's behaviour. Some of the things your child does may also be things that all children do. For example, jumping up and down in excitement is a common behaviour among children. But most children will only do this occasionally, when there is a very real reason to be very excited. A child with ASD may jump up and down continually and incessantly for no apparent reason. They may jump for hours at a time. So, if you tell someone that your child jumps up and down a lot, they may dismiss you, saying that it is normal for a child to jump. They may believe that you are being anxious for no reason.

Most people are so ignorant still of what autism actually is that unless your child fits their stereotypical picture of autism, they will not see signs of it in your child. You, too, may never have met a child with autism or know a family with a child on the spectrum so you will be equally ignorant of what the condition means. If your child has the more classic, severe form of autism they will be diagnosed before or around the age of three. At this stage, you may not yet have been exposed to the numbers of children that you will later come across in various educational settings. You may still be in that cocoon of post-natal mothers who meet regularly and discuss their children's progress. Your child may be at a small nursery with limited numbers of children. So perhaps you will have never met a child who has autism. If you have a school-age child, you may well have come across other children at nursery or school who do have a diagnosis of ASD. You will perhaps have more of an idea about what autism might entail. Every child is unique and in every child the symptoms and severity of any symptoms will differ. So, even having met a number of children with autism, you may still not have any real idea of what it may mean to you and your family.

Your child may have started to fall behind and not be achieving the milestones that other children in their peer group have acquired such as speech and language.

My twins were still not talking by the time they were diagnosed, so by then we had started to realize that something was not quite right. But we would never have dreamt that our boys would be labelled with such a serious disability as autism.

Clarification of Disability
It could be that the diagnosis comes as a *sort* of relief, not a real relief at all, but if you have been worrying about your child for a while and those around you have not acknowledged or taken your concerns seriously, you may feel some relief that you have not been imagining it all along.

When our third son started to display some signs of autism similar to those of his older twin brothers (both already diagnosed with classic autism) everyone including health professionals and family thought we

---

were being neurotic and anxious when we voiced our concerns about him. Again, we were fed reassuring, delaying tactics such as his hearing problems and glue ear. People suggested that perhaps he wasn't talking because his older brothers weren't talking very much either at that time. Of course, first-born children talk without older siblings to learn from, but in our case this small fact went unnoticed. It took us a while to get people to take our concerns seriously, perhaps also partly due to the fact that his development had been totally normal until two years of age. If it was hard for us who already had two children diagnosed with autism and who knew the signs, how hard is it for others to be taken seriously?

So, you may take small comfort in the fact that you are not going mad and imagining things and that hopefully people will start to take you seriously at last. You may be very anxious and very emotional but that does not mean that your worries are invalid. It can be very hard to keep your emotions in check during the early stages of diagnosis, some questions may be very upsetting. Some or most of the things you may be told about your child are not what you want to hear so, of course, you will be upset. Sometimes, you need to try and hold your emotions in while you are actually having a consultation with a specialist. Your appointment time is limited and you want to try to get as much as possible from it. If you cry and become very upset, then you may come away not having asked all the questions you wanted to ask. If you can make a list of questions before a consultation, this will help you to maximize your time and it can also help you to remain focused. Inevitably, if you are upset, your mind may go blank and you will only remember what you wanted to ask sometime after the consultation when it is too late.

I have had many appointments where I have held myself together and managed to get as much information as I could, only to burst into tears as soon as I have left the room. I don't withhold my tears. I just try to manage where and when I cry.

Acceptance by One or by Both Parents
Between parents themselves there can be issues in agreeing together about your child's problems. Sadly, some parents almost turn a blind eye to what is happening to their son or daughter. They

just cannot handle the pain that it causes them to even imagine that there is anything wrong or different about their child. So, one parent may be in denial while the other parent accepts and acknowledges the issues. One parent may believe or wish to believe that autism is a fairly minor problem that will go away if not given too much attention. They may think that perhaps the professionals have got it wrong and everything will be alright in the end. Fathers may not be able to accept that their son may not do the things that they had been planning on doing with them. Of course, parents do not necessarily wish a replica of their own life for their child, but all parents want to be able to offer as much as they had in their own childhoods and ideally more than they had or experienced. The idea that the destiny of you, your child and your family unit has changed enormously is a very hard concept to accept.

If parents are not equally able to acknowledge a diagnosis, then an already difficult family situation can turn into an even worse one. Your relationship with each other is vital at this point as you are the only ones who can really understand what the other is going through. If one of you does not accept the situation, then your relationship will come under huge strain, which is the last thing you need at this point. You need to be able to support one another in caring for your child. If you feel that you are not united in your acknowledgement and feelings about your child's diagnosis, then try and seek some professional help for your relationship sooner rather than later if you can. Along with all the appointments for your child, it might be very hard to factor in time for yourselves, but in the long run, if you can stay together in a united and loving relationship, it will be so much better for everyone. Some parents get so tied up in their child and their child's issues that they almost forget about the relationship that they were in with their partner before the diagnosis hit. A couple can grow apart almost without noticing it. When a woman has a baby, it is often said that the baby becomes all-consuming to her and her partner can feel quite neglected for a while, but this does not usually last long enough to cause a problem in the relationship. A child with special needs can take so much of your time and energy on an ongoing basis and can also become all consuming. If you allow this to happen, it may also cause a permanent rift between you and your partner. Your child needs you, but so does your partner, who will also be grieving and perhaps be experiencing shock just as you are, about your child's future.

Statistically, there is a higher incidence in breakdown of marriage among families with a child with special needs owing to the strain that this situation puts on couples. If you know this in advance, it should act as a warning to be aware of and not as something inevitable. Perhaps if all parents were offered help with their relationships around the time their child was diagnosed, then this statistic could be lowered.

The Shock of a Diagnosis

Again, the fact that most disabilities in children these days are either known before the child is born or usually soon after birth means that autism is one of the few lifelong disabilities that is not apparent early on. This does not alter the pain any parent will have on hearing that their child has a disability, but the fact that it sneaks up on you after a few years of normal childhood development can make the diagnosis even harder to embrace.

Our third son was talking and doing everything he should by two years old when suddenly it was as if a light had switched off and he started to lose all his speech and eye contact and then to withdraw into himself. This was a dreadful shock when we all believed that he was going to be unaffected by the autism his brothers have. We also had to suffer some very cruel comments at the time from people who couldn't understand why we were so shocked and so upset. They seemed to think that we should have known it was coming. We were told things like 'Well, it will be easier this time; you know what you have to do.' In actual fact, it was harder the third time around as we did, indeed, know exactly what we would have to do. Everyone's circumstances are different, but everyone will feel pain on hearing the diagnosis of autism for their child. The fact that you already have children with ASD does not diminish the fact that another of your children also has it, nor does it make the pain any easier to bear.

Holding onto Hope

Try not to despair on hearing that your child has autism. Do not listen to any negative stuff that people will try to tell you. No one can predict how your child will be in the future, how well they may do and what it is possible for them to achieve. Hope is crucial and you need to remain hopeful for your child's future. A total cure or recovery may not be possible, but there is a great deal of improvement that can be made and do not allow anyone to tell you otherwise. You will, of course, want to find out as much as you can about your child's condition and what you can do to help them. There is a great deal of information on the internet that you can access, and it can be hard to know where to start. There are many support groups online and forums, and even blogs from a parent's perspective. There are also professional and charitable organizations that have websites and offer a wealth of information.

Families have such different experiences and each child is different in the way in which autism affects them, so be careful of what you read and what you believe. It will certainly not all apply to you or your child. People will tell you about someone they know with a child with autism, or that they have heard of a miracle cure. They may recount experiences that do not apply to you in any way. People like to get their information in varied ways. Going online means you can get infinite sources of information from all around the world and at any time of day or night. Forums online also mean that you can ask or answer questions whenever you have a few minutes spare to do so. The difficulty is that it is hard to know which information to trust. Some people prefer to obtain information from others who may already have experience of looking after a child with autism. Their experience may not mirror your own and their child may have very different needs, so this is not always the easiest option it may appear to be. When you have only recently got a diagnosis, although you will want to know more, try to avoid reading too much at first. The internet and all the forums can be overwhelming until you decide which ones resonate with you.

On hearing that my twins had autism, I went straight to the library to see what I could read. The first book I picked up was so negative and said something about parents having ridiculously unreal expectations that their child would ever work in the future. I stopped reading right there and then, and didn't pick up another book for months. I didn't get into online forums for many years as I didn't really have the time or inclination. Other people's experiences were not necessarily mine. Perhaps in one sense, I didn't want to know what the future held for my boys. In that way the future was left open to possibility. I am glad that I didn't try to look too far into the future because in many ways the boys are much more able than I would ever have been able to imagine. They are certainly doing much better than the professionals thought was likely. To me, they are proof that early intervention is key to any child's future.

You may wish only to talk personally to other parents and carers in the same situation as you are. However, as you will find, autism is very time-consuming and other parents may have limited time in which to talk as they, too, will be very busy looking after their own child. Try to respect this, no matter how desperate you are to talk with them. Some organizations, such as the local branches of the NAS (National Autistic Society), may have parents willing to be contacted about certain issues. Although people who have just been given a new diagnosis for their child are usually desperate for support from other parents, try to remember that other parents have very busy lives of their own. They may have been through the diagnosis stage and have moved on, but they may well be in a new stage that is equally demanding and stressful, such as going to tribunal to fight for the educational provision for their child. Usually, though, you will find other parents will do what they can to help you and will try to make time to talk or offer advice.

Coming to Terms with a Diagnosis

First, before you listen to anyone else, you yourself need to come to terms with the fact that your child has been given a life-changing diagnosis. You may not want to tell your family or friends for a while – at least, not until you know how you feel about it and are strong enough to share your news. You may be part of a very supportive family, in which case you will want to tell them straightaway and gain comfort and support from them. They may help you to come to terms with your child's diagnosis and be willing to do whatever they can to help you and your child. This, of course, would be the situation in an ideal world, but, sadly, not all families are like this. If you have any fears that your family may not say the right things, try to delay telling them until you feel more able to cope with their reaction. Geographically, you may live a long distance from your parents or siblings, so they will not be able to offer practical support in the form of physical help on a day-to-day basis. Nevertheless, an understanding relative or good friend you can talk to on the phone may be just as valuable.

All your hopes and dreams for your child will collapse as you hear the diagnosis. Even before your child was born, you will have had aspirations of the life ahead for you and your child. Both your life and the life you expected for your child have been altered with that one word: autism. If your child has regressed to reach the point at which they are at, you will be mourning the child your child previously was. It can feel like your child was fine one day and you lost them overnight. They may have been talking and playing, well and happy, and then suddenly all is lost and your child is bewildered and unable to communicate and somehow not the child you knew. It can take a long time for you to accept this. You will keep waiting for the child you knew to return. If your child has not regressed, but has slowly slipped behind in their normal development, the diagnosis will still be a huge shock.

If you can, try your very hardest to stay positive about your child's future. There is so much you can do; you can make a real difference to the outcome for your child. Do not listen to anyone who tries to tell you that there is nothing much you can do. Health professionals are often negative about expectations for your child. Partly, this is because they do not want to raise your hopes and partly perhaps because they know that funding and accessing what your child needs can be hugely demanding for you. You may not be eligible for funding all the therapies that your child needs. Outsiders may not wish to put extra pressure and stress on you by telling you that you need to do all the things for your child, which perhaps you cannot afford to provide. So, professionals and others may try to keep your expectations low in order to protect you. What you most need to hear is that there is a great deal of hope and that with early intervention your child's prognosis can improve enormously. Total recovery is probably not a realistic expectation but you will be surprised over time what you and your child can achieve.

But ... you will only be able to help your child if you believe that you can. You are the most important person in your child's life and you can make a huge difference. Even if you don't have the available money for many of the therapies, there are ways of accessing funding and the help that you need.

Getting Emotional Support

Sometimes, getting on with helping your child as soon as you can helps you to deal with the emotional side of things. You may almost become too busy to sit and dwell too long on how you feel. Knowledge is empowering, the more you know and understand about your child's condition, the better you will be able to help. If you have a bad day, try not to be too hard on yourself; we all have bad days. If you like to read, try to find some uplifting stories of children who have improved way beyond their parents' original expectations. Perhaps join an internet support group where you can ask questions from people who have been through or who are going through right now what you are going through. There may be a local support group for parents whose children have autism. Try to get in touch. Other parents will give you hope and often offer more support than your own family can as they understand your situation so much better. They may also be a good source of information and save you a lot of time researching everything on your own.

Family Views

In the way that some parents are not able to accept their own child's diagnosis of autism, so, too, grandparents may be unable to understand their grandchild's condition fully. For years, they may have blamed your parenting skills for your child's behaviour as inevitably your child will have some behavioural problems. To outsiders, the way your child behaves will often be termed as 'naughty' and an indication that you have let your child get away with things and have not disciplined them properly. When you learn more about your child's diagnosis and the fact that these behaviours are not your fault, you may feel some relief. Your parents and others, however, may still think that somehow you should be able to control your child better and that the diagnosis of autism is almost an excuse for bad behaviour. It is very hard for any parent to be criticized for their parenting skills by their own parents and even harder to take when you know that it really is not your parenting skills that are to blame.

I am not alone in finding it so much harder to be judged by a member of my family than by a stranger. Somehow you expect your family to understand your child's condition and why they do the things that they do. It is much easier to be criticized by a stranger you can dismiss and try to forget about than it is by your own family with whom you have to maintain a relationship.

Grandparents suffer in their own right, too. They have expectations of being a grandparent and all the joy that entails. They have hopes for your children, maybe hopes for things that you or your partner did not succeed in doing and which they now wish for their grandchild. They may suffer the loss of not being the grandparent they expected to be, which is similar to the loss you experience in not being a parent in the way that you expected or imagined you would be. Of course, they are still your child's grandparent and you will hope that they will continue to love your child in the same way that you still love your child. Many will manage this and be able to adapt to the new reality. Sadly, some will not adapt, mainly because of their own personalities and expectations. You may find that if they have other grandchildren without disabilities or problems that they will lavish more care and attention on them and back away from your child. Of course, this rejection will hit you doubly hard as these other grandchildren will also be part of your own family and you will have to witness this favouritism.

Do not be too disheartened by other people's attitudes. You will meet some wonderful people along the way while doing your best for your child. There are many teachers and therapists who really do want to make a difference to your child's life. Not many people work in the area of special needs just because they need a job or for the financial rewards; most are doing it because they care. You may also be lucky to find volunteers and charities who will help you and your child unpaid. Having a child with special needs can be expensive enough as it is, so anyone offering their services for free is to be appreciated.

Try to stay positive and remain confident that you can truly help your child. There is a lot of research in progress and new ideas for both medical and educational help are being developed all the time. You really do not know how your child will develop as he or she grows up and you should not place any limits on what progress they can make. No professional will be able to predict accurately how your child might be in five or ten years' time or even how they will function as an adult with autism. It is even hard to predict whether a child will acquire functional language or what level of communication they will be able to reach. The fact that you do not know how far your child could progress will keep you motivated to do all that you can to maximize their potential. There are so many different therapies available now to help your child, your only obstacle should be how to fund them and which ones to choose.

Once you have a diagnosis and you have accepted it, you need to get to work!

3

COEXISTING CONDITIONS AND THE MEDICAL SIDE OF AUTISM

Autistic spectrum disorder (ASD) is a label for a complex list of conditions and disorders. Your child may display many or just a few of the criteria necessary for this diagnosis to be applied to them. When you meet other parents and their children, you will realize how broad the label ASD is and how very different the children diagnosed with this label can be.

Classic Autism
Children at the more severe end of the spectrum will be probably be diagnosed at a much younger age because their symptoms are more obvious and more extreme. For example, a child who has no spoken language should be identified as having a communication disorder by the age of three. Children with more severe symptoms were previously labelled as having classic or Kanner's autism, which means autism that is identified in early childhood. Sometimes it is also known as childhood autism, but unfortunately this term implies that the condition may be only childhood-related and that these children will somehow grow out of it and therefore no longer be autistic in adulthood. It is now thought that some symptoms of autism may be detectable at a very young age, i.e. from around twelve months. There are research programmes currently looking at very young siblings who already have a family history of autism to try to establish how early some of the symptoms of autism may be present and detectable.

Asperger's Syndrome

A child at the higher end of the spectrum (for example, with a milder form of autism like Asperger's syndrome) may not be identified until much later in childhood or even into adulthood. In the case of a child with Asperger's it may be that you have known for a while that their behaviour is somehow different from their peers, but it may take many years for them to be diagnosed as such. There may be no obvious issue, e.g. language delay, that would alert you to the fact that your child needs additional help. A child with Asperger's will have problems that are more to do with social interaction and behaviours not usually picked up until school age and, as such, it may not become apparent for quite a few years later that your child has Asperger's.

Until recently, autism and Asperger's were two different diagnoses. In 2013, the *Diagnostic and Statistical Manual 5* (DSM) of the American Psychiatric Association (APA) was published. This stated that officially, they are both now under the umbrella term of autism spectrum disorders. Although the DSM is produced by the APA, it influences diagnosis across the world. Anyone with a previous diagnosis will not lose that diagnosis, but from now the diagnosis will only be that of ASD, whatever the level of autism a child is deemed as having. This is intended to aid people in obtaining a diagnosis and therefore to get the help they may need, but in some ways it has caused more confusion. Unofficially, children will probably still continue to be labelled and separated into the two original categories. Certainly, most parents are quite clear about which label applies to their child.

No child will fit an exact criterion. This is true even of identical twins where the chances of autism in both twins is very high but not totally 100 per cent, which implies that there has to be an environmental influence and that it is not down purely to genetics. Identical twins where one or both twins have autism are very important in research because of this anomaly. In non-identical twins the chances of both twins being affected by autism are the same or slightly higher than with another sibling.

Every human being is an individual and personality and physical make-up also has to be taken into consideration. Autism is not a quantifiable condition and cannot be exactly measured. A child with a hearing or visual problem may be given a precise measurement that states exactly what their visual or hearing deficit is and their results can usually be plotted on a chart or scale. There are no figures or precise measurements that can be applied in autism. Even if your child completes a range of tests, these will not necessarily place them at a certain level as your child may perform higher in one test than another and there is no single definitive test. Social interaction cannot be quantified, also.

No Medical Tests for Autism

From a medical point of view, autism cannot be diagnosed with any specific medical criteria such as blood tests or brain scans, so the diagnosis has to be made on observational factors and not finite physical ones. It is often a developmental paediatrician who makes the diagnosis, although it is not currently seen as a medical condition. After the initial diagnosis, you will probably not see a paediatrician again as your child's care will then become the responsibility of the educational system and not the health system. You may, of course, be referred to specific specialist doctors if your child additionally has a medical problem that needs care and treatment, e.g. epilepsy or diabetes. There are no autism doctors who actively treat autism in mainstream medicine. There are paediatric neurologists or psychiatrists who may diagnose autism, but they do not treat autism as it is not currently a curable medical condition. They may treat some symptoms of autism, such as extreme anxiety, with medication. However, there are many therapeutic options to help aspects of autism. Examples of these include behavioural programmes that modify your child's behaviour, which can do a great deal to lessen the symptoms or severity of your child's autism.

Autism Cannot be Quantified

Autism can never be precisely measured, or sometimes even diagnosed accurately, because of the wide range of issues and problems that it can cause. You may be able to get a speech and language assessment giving an approximate score analysing your child's language. This might give them an age equivalent language level, but as the tests are devised for children without autism, they are still not a true level of your child's ability. Language can be acquired in a different way from other children so that your child may have sophisticated language in some areas but not in others. They may have a higher level of receptive (understanding) language than expressive (that they are able to speak back). In rare instances, a few children who are essentially non-verbal have been found to be able to type and communicate via computers using sophisticated language.

Your child may be advanced in some areas of development and delayed in others. They may be having a bad day when the tests are carried out or be unable to respond properly to testing due to outside factors affecting them. If they are noise sensitive, they may be overwhelmed and unable to cooperate. Tests are often performed in an unknown environment, which straight away will put many children at a disadvantage. Even if your child is assessed at home, it will often be by a stranger whose presence may be disturbing. If your child is made to wait for too long in a strange waiting-room, you may rapidly lose any attention your child may have had if the test had been carried out promptly on your arrival.

I needed an occupational therapy assessment for tribunal, which I could ill afford at the time. It was private and very expensive, and because my son was kept waiting for over an hour, he was too tired and upset to do any of the tests. The subsequent report we received was so inaccurate that we couldn't even submit it to tribunal.

Your child may not perform well for someone they have never met. Although they are capable of doing a test, they may not understand what is being asked of them due to their communication problems. Your child's test results can be heavily influenced by the tester's own experience in gaining the confidence of a child, being able to impart what they actually require your child to do and their level of knowledge of children with autism. Too many factors like this affect any testing and analysis that your child may need.

All the psychological tests and cognitive tests may just indicate your child's mood and ability on that single occasion. There are a battery of written tests like the Vineland Adaptive Behaviour Scale, which scores for social abilities and looks at your child's ability to learn new skills or cope with environmental changes. Some of these tests can be completed by the parents or by other people who know your child well and so your child's ability to cooperate is not required. The results may help professionals working with your child to understand some of the problems which you and your child may have with everyday living.

Genetic Factors of Autism

About the only tests with any total accuracy may be blood tests, which in themselves can be hugely stressful for your child. At least the results are absolute, although it is only really chromosomal disorders such as Fragile X that can be detected in blood tests. There are no markers for autism in blood so, for most children, a blood test will not yield any answers

Fragile X

The leading known genetic cause of autism is Fragile X, which accounts for approximately 5 per cent of children with autism. This is due to a mutation on the X chromosome. Boys have only a single X and a single Y chromosome, so if they inherit this condition they are more likely to be affected than girls who carry two Xs. In a girl, if only one X is affected, the other will be undamaged, which may result in the girl being a carrier of the condition but otherwise unaffected. Some girls will have symptoms as a result of the damaged X, but usually only a third will have learning difficulties. Therefore, more boys are affected by Fragile X than girls. The symptoms of Fragile X are very similar to those of autism, but only a small number of children with this condition do actually have autism. Fragile X can be diagnosed by a blood test developed in 1991, and your child may be tested for this condition when they are going through the diagnosis process for autism.

Down's Syndrome

Some children may have another known genetic condition along-side their autism. Children with Down's syndrome are now known to have a higher incidence of autism than the general population; around 10–15 per cent of children with Down's syndrome now have a diagnosis of autism. This knowledge is fairly recent and previously any additional problems a child with Down's syndrome had were seen as part of the Down's syndrome diagnosis. Again, children's abilities with this condition can vary enormously with very different levels of learning difficulty and acquisition of speech in the same way that all children on the autistic spectrum vary.

Tuberous Sclerosis

Approximately 2–4 per cent of children with autism have Tuberous Sclerosis (TS). This is a genetic disorder in which tubers or lesions grow in various parts of the body, but especially in the brain. Although the majority of children with TS are not diagnosed with autism, around 43–61 per cent of children with TS have symptoms of autism. Autism in these children may be diagnosed at a later age due to the progression of the disease, which may in time cause autism alongside other symptoms.

There is a high incidence of epilepsy among the autism population. This is discussed further on page 83.

Apart from these known identifiable medical conditions there are also other coexisting disorders that many children with ASD have as well and which are also classified as being autistic spectrum disorders, such as dyspraxia and ADHD.

Dyspraxia

Dyspraxia is a form of developmental coordination disorder (DCD). It is in the category of neurodevelopmental disorders in the APA's *Diagnostic and Statistical Manual of Mental Disorders* and is classified as a motor disorder. It is lifelong and cannot be cured, but there are many things that can be done to make life easier for those who have it.

It affects fine and or gross motor coordination. This may cause problems with balance and timing. It can also cause difficulties in spatial awareness (proprioception), which is the ability of the brain to process where different parts of the body, e.g. the limbs are. This can cause clumsiness where children with dyspraxia often knock over objects or bump into objects and people. This clumsiness is often the only problem that people recognize as being part of having dyspraxia.

However, there are other unseen issues that children with this condition have problems with. These include problems with planning. They may not be able to follow and remember instructions in sequence. They may have problems in organizing and carrying out everyday movements and procedures. A child with dyspraxia, for example, may need help to dress themselves. Not only will they have motor problems doing up buttons and zips, but they may also have issues with dressing in the correct order and need help in putting their clothes on in the right sequence. So a child with dyspraxia may put their clothes on back to front, for example.

Poor short-term memory can also be an issue. They may not be able to remember more than one instruction at a time. For instance, if asked to go upstairs and carry out a task, they may go upstairs and then forget why they are there as they have forgotten the task. They may start doing something else and not come back downstairs again. There is an increased likelihood of them losing things, too, as they cannot remember where they put something.

There is also a condition known as *developmental verbal dyspraxia*. A child may have difficulty in learning to talk because they have problems controlling the speech organs, such as the lips and tongue, to make certain sounds. So a child with autism who additionally has verbal dyspraxia will be doubly hampered in learning to talk.

Children with dyspraxia can be greatly helped by therapists such as occupational therapists (OTs), physiotherapists and SLTs. OTs often go into schools to help with issues around handwriting and pencil grip, throwing and catching balls, core-body strength and many other issues. They can often provide equipment, both at home and at school, and exercises to help with motor skills.

A child with poor memory skills may be helped with visual prompts such as photos in a sequence to help them remember the order in which they need to carry out a task such as dressing. They will also benefit from routine as certain tasks can then become learned. A child with autism who does not like change will find learning new routines even harder if they also have dyspraxia.

Attention Deficit Hyperactivity Disorder (ADHD)

As its name implies, this condition causes problems with inattention, hyperactivity and acting impulsively to a degree not appropriate for the child's age. Not every child with ADHD has all the symptoms, though. In the UK, the National Institute for Health and Care Excellence (NICE) has guidelines for the diagnosis and management of ADHD.

Based on the criteria provided in the *Diagnostic and Statistical Manual* of the APA, there are three sub-types of ADHD that cover the symptoms of ADHD presented by a child:

- Predominantly inattentive (ADHD-PI): such children are easily distracted, forgetful, disorganized and have difficulty completing tasks. This category is often called *attention deficit disorder* (ADD).
- Predominantly hyperactive-impulsive: such children are hyperactive, restless, have difficulty waiting and remaining seated, have immature behaviour and may also be destructive.
- A combination of both ADHD-PI and hyper-active-impulsive.

While many people in the population may show some signs of these symptoms to varying degrees, it is only those with a significant severity of symptoms who will actually be diagnosed with ADHD.

ADHD is the most common behavioural disorder in the UK. Various estimates suggest it affects around 5 per cent of school-age children in the UK. Around three times more boys than girls are diagnosed with the condition. To be diagnosed within the criteria of the DSM 5, symptoms must be observed in multiple settings for six months or more and to a degree that is much greater than others of the same age.

Some research has shown that 30–80 per cent of children diagnosed with autism also have ADHD and that more than half of the children diagnosed with ADHD meet the diagnostic criteria for autism spectrum disorders. So there is a strong link and increased likelihood that a child diagnosed with autism may also have ADHD as a coexisting disorder.

Young children with autism often display signs of hyperactivity and inattention, particularly when reaching school age, but this may lessen with time as they mature. Therefore, an ADHD diagnosis may not be appropriate until a child is older and if the symptoms still persist. Because autism is seen to be a more significant disability, that is usually the primary diagnosis given at an early age, and a diagnosis of ADHD may not be made at the same time or may not be deemed as necessary. If a child is assessed as having special educational needs because of their autism, any symptoms or problems they have should be addressed by their educational plan so an additional diagnosis may not be particularly useful or necessary at an early stage.

Of my four boys, two have ADHD in addition to their autism. One of the boys was formally diagnosed at around the age of seven as he needed medication for his condition, which was greatly affecting his ability to learn. He was unable to pay attention, sit still or concentrate on anything for any length of time. With the medication, he learned to read and write within a short period of time and we were also able to manage his behaviour better. Within a year or so, we were able to take him off the medication. He was also having intensive behavioural therapy at the same time.

Our other son has never had a formal diagnosis of ADHD as his educational needs are met by his statement of special educational needs. He has more verbal language than his brother and so we were able to manage his behaviour a little better without medication. Therefore, there seems to be no reason to have another diagnosis added.

It may be quite difficult to distinguish between the two diagnoses if your child has both autism and ADHD.

ADHD is not considered to be a learning disability but around 20–30 per cent of children with ADHD do have learning disabilities.

Treatment for ADHD

Treatment for ADHD usually involves behaviour therapy of some kind. This is often behaviour management that may use rewards to try to help your child manage the ADHD themselves. They will need strategies to try and combat their impulsive behaviour. In reality, this can be much harder than it appears on paper. A child who is impulsive reacts to a situation almost instantly, i.e. without thinking about it at all. While others would weigh up a situation and whether or not they should go ahead and do something, a child with ADHD will not stop to think and will just go ahead and do it. In later years, these are the sort of children who potentially end up in serious trouble for crimes such as setting fire to a building. Their sense of what is morally acceptable may become blurred as their need to carry out an impulsive action takes over from any other logical thought. So those children with severe issues in this area need intensive help at a young age to prevent them growing up and causing harm to themselves and others. As a parent, it can be a huge worry if your child is very impulsive. From a young age, you will be judged by your child's behaviour, especially as they will appear simply to be 'naughty' to others who may wonder aloud about how badly behaved your child is.

By school age, your child may also be labelled as 'naughty' and be judged by this from the start of their school years. They can be a poor role model for other children, who may admire them for their daring acts. Young children have ended up being excluded from school in severe circumstances, so it is vital to try to address these problems as early as possible.

Alongside behaviour therapy for your child, you may be offered parent training, either alone or in groups. This will offer you specific ways of talking and playing with your child as well as effective techniques to help you to help them manage their behaviour. Such training will also teach you how to react to their behaviour and ways to defuse difficult situations or even prevent them from occurring.

Those children with inattentive ADHD are more a problem to themselves than to others. They will have a much reduced ability to learn due to their inability to concentrate and pay attention. In a child with autism who desperately needs to learn important skills like speech and language, this inability to attend compounds the whole situation. It is already hard to teach a child with autism who may have other issues, such as sensory or motor problems, that hamper learning. Adding ADHD to these other disorders makes teaching skills to these children even harder.

If your child is able to acquire some language or to read instructions, then you have a basic structure with which to teach them other skills. If they cannot stay still long enough to learn these basics, it may be very difficult to move on to further learning.

A reward system that rewards a child for keeping their attention focused for a limited time may be beneficial. A child will learn to do a short task and then receive a reward for completing it. This time can then be very gradually increased. It may be done via a verbal countdown of time to begin with, or even a clock with an alarm when they can manage longer periods of time.

An OT may be of significant help and support for you and your child. Your child may need a sensory cushion to sit on, which stimulates them and enables them to sit still for longer periods. They may advise the use of small toys or objects to handle and play with while they are sitting still and perhaps watching or listening to someone. This may be more relevant in a child of school age to help them to sit for longer periods of time in a classroom.

A change in diet can also help a child who has ADHD. Sugar and food colouring or additives may aggravate symptoms. You may need to remove all these from your child's diet and then experiment with giving them one item, such as something containing a high level of sugar and then noting any reaction they may have to it. Keeping a food diary in this way may be helpful as you may be able to pinpoint certain behaviours correlating with specific foods eaten on that day. A dietician may be able to advise on dietary measures that could reduce the symptoms of ADHD.

Sometimes it may be necessary for your child to be prescribed medication if it is felt that their symptoms are severe and affecting their lives. In some cases, medication can mean that your child is able to learn important life skills. Medication will only be prescribed by a qualified paediatric (children's) doctor. The medication cannot cure ADHD, but will lessen the symptoms so that your child can concentrate better and feel calmer. Your child may need to take the medication every day or sometimes, just on school days. There may be side-effects so your child should be monitored carefully by the prescribing doctor.

The use of medication in ADHD is often controversial. Some believe that too many children have been prescribed medication in order to make life easier for their parents. Some children may be seen as being overly boisterous and very active and, in fact, with more exercise their 'symptoms' may be addressed. In some countries the level of medication and diagnosis of ADHD is very high. There are even some professionals who question the existence of the condition at all. Therefore, diagnosis should not be assumed too easily. A child should be observed in different settings, and other adults, such as carers or teachers, should also be included in the assessment. Sometimes children's behaviour is much worse for certain caregivers for various reasons. This needs to be clarified before a diagnosis is made.

But for a child who already has a diagnosis of autism, the likelihood of them also having ADHD as a coexisting disorder is quite high, so in these children, the ADHD is likely to be of a physical cause and not due to other factors such as poor parenting or unhealthy lifestyles. In the same way that you are not the cause of your child's autism, you are also not the cause of their ADHD. Most of your child's symptoms will be present due to their disorder and not to anything you have or have not done. But, like autism, there is a lot you can do to help your child once you have a definite diagnosis.

Obsessive Compulsive Disorder (OCD)

There are other disorders that are also thought to be linked with autism, such as OCD. There seems to be a higher incidence of these disorders coexisting with autism than there does in the general population as a whole. This may be due to a genetic link, but has yet to be proven.

In OCD, a child or adult will have extreme repetitive behaviours. Many children with autism show repetitive behaviours and repeatedly do the same actions over and over again. Although sometimes people may assume from this that such a child has the symptoms of OCD, their repetitive behaviour may, in fact, be simply due to their autism, the difference being that in OCD the individual carries out repetitive actions because of anxiety. e.g. repeatedly washing their hands because they are anxious about germs. In autism there may be no anxiety involved and a child is more usually 'stimming' or carrying out an action over and over again because it gives them a form of pleasure to do so. Sometimes, a child with autism will show signs of repeated actions due to severe anxiety and then they may be classified as having symptoms of OCD. As with autism and ADHD, behaviour management can be very useful. A child may also be offered cognitive behaviour therapy, but this may not be very viable for a child who is non-verbal or has severe problems due to their autism.

Learning Disability

Autism is generally understood to be a developmental, behavioural or learning disability. Children diagnosed with autism may also fit into the category of having a specific learning difficulty that covers problems such as dyslexia and dyspraxia. Alternatively, they may be classified as having a learning disability depending on the severity of their issues and problems. A more severe learning disability may also be known as *global development delay*.

If your child's problems are mostly behavioural or in the area of social interaction, then they may not easily fit into any category. This can make obtaining recognition and help for them much harder. They may meet the social impairment criteria for an autism diagnosis, but still may not be seen as having an additional educational need. Many children fit into several categories but will still be given the all-encompassing diagnosis of autism. So the fact that autism covers such a wide variety of symptoms and varies greatly in its presentation makes it difficult to categorize it into one type of disability.

The dictionary definition of a learning disability is 'a condition giving rise to learning difficulties, especially when not associated with physical disability'.

'Learning disability' is the term that the Department of Health use within its policy and practice documents. In *Valuing People* (2001), the Department of Health describes a 'learning disability' as a:

- significantly reduced ability to understand new or complex information, to learn new skills
- reduced ability to cope independently which starts before adulthood with lasting effects on development.

Autism and Genetics

Some research suggests that autism may have a strong genetic link. In a family with a child with autism, the chances of another sibling also being on the autistic spectrum is increased. Although the risk of another child in the same family also being affected by autism varies depending on which expert you consult, it is often given as a 20 per cent increased risk as a minimum estimate.

There are some families where one or both parents have also been identified as being on the autistic spectrum themselves or where other members of the wider family unit are affected. Sometimes, after a child is diagnosed, the parents then look to themselves and realize that one of them may have undiagnosed symptoms, which means that they too may be on the autistic spectrum. In other families, there may be members of the wider family affected, such as cousins or uncles or aunts. Some families will have members of different generations affected and a strong family link to relatives being on the autistic spectrum. They may have varying degrees of spectrum disorders ranging from high-functioning autism (previously known as Asperger's syndrome), which in previous generations may not have been diagnosed, to more severely affected individuals who again may have been given a different label before autism was identified as a condition.

Other families may have no previous history of any member of the family being affected by autism in any form. So might there be some autism due to genetic, hereditary factors and some due to environmental causes? Or, in fact, is autism caused by a combination of both an inherited risk and an environmental factor?

We were seen by the genetics departments of two London teaching hospitals after all three of my sons had been diagnosed with autism. The first consultant suggested our risk rate was around 50 per cent of having another child with autism. We sought a second opinion and were told by this second consultant that our chances would always be 20 per cent however many children we went on to have. Twenty per cent seemed a low enough risk so we decided to go ahead and have another child. Of course, a risk factor is only ever that – an educated guess – and we went on to have another son who was also diagnosed with autism at an early age. We wouldn't be without him; he is a ray of sunshine in all our lives, but it shows that in different families perhaps different genetics apply.

The problem with the genetic theory is that no specific gene has yet been identified that could be solely implicated in the role of autism. There may, in fact, be multiple genes involved so that autism is not inherited from one parent but from a combination of genetic factors from both parents. Even if it is proven that there is a genetic cause, we still do not know what the trigger or triggers are that cause autism to develop in those children with a genetic susceptibility. Could the triggers be environmental, dietary, due to allergy, or even caused by a virus? Is it genetic and therefore inevitable from birth that a child will go on to develop autism? Or is there a susceptibility that may or may not be triggered at some point by one of many different factors? Is a child in the womb already destined to have autism or does the possibility of it happen after birth?

The number of children diagnosed with autism is increasing all the time. Some may argue that increased awareness of the condition is causing more children to be diagnosed than previously, or that the condition has always existed but been called by various other names. But even if the numbers are adjusted for children who may have previously been diagnosed with a different label, such as learning difficulties, it is still true to say that the number of children diagnosed with autism is increasing year on year. Most children with severe autism will be less likely in the future to have children of their own, so from a genetic point of view, this should mean that numbers decrease, but only time will tell if this will be so.

Children with severe autism are often born to parents who do not appear to have any aspects of autism themselves. So, are the traits and signs of autism more obvious in some families and perhaps silent in others? Is it possible that some parents carry the genetic risk while not having autism themselves like in many other inherited conditions? If two parents carry the risk factor, does the combination of their genes together cause an increased risk of autism in their children?

Autism is a spectrum and does not have exact criteria to measure how 'autistic' any child is, so it is never possible to say where on the spectrum a particular child is. There are so many symptoms and a child may have deficits in one area but excel in another. Trying to define whether a child is so called low-functioning or high-functioning is very subjective, but children are often placed into these rather vague categories. Those deemed as being more severely affected have usually been diagnosed at a young age, perhaps at the age of two or three. They are probably not talking or understanding language at this age, exhibiting unusual patterns of behaviour and are often very restless. They will receive a diagnosis at a younger age than those with less severe problems. As these children mature, some will do better than others in terms of improvement in many areas of life such as language, behaviour and social interaction. The ones who improve more may be reassessed at an older age as being high-functioning while those who retain the more severe aspects of autism may still be termed as being low-functioning.

Pain in a Child with Autism

Many medical illnesses lie hidden and unseen within the body. Most people are able to describe what sort of pain they are in, perhaps where the pain is located and how severe it is. A child with no communication skills may be unable to let you know that they are in any discomfort. This may mean that their medical issues are not addressed until much later than they would be in a child who is able to communicate and tell you what is wrong.

Extreme pain may present as a tantrum or in the form of a child self-harming (for example, hitting or biting themselves). In this instance, a child may be trying to distract themselves from pain in one area by causing a different type of pain in another. Because they may be unable to communicate either verbally or non-verbally that they are in physical pain, their behaviour may be attributed to the fact that they have autism and thus be dismissed as just another symptom of their autism. For example, a child with a severe headache may perhaps repeatedly hit themselves on the head, or hit their head against a wall in an effort to relieve the pain. A severe headache may also cause them to scream or to get very upset when they hear loud noises. This type of behaviour may often be due to sensory issues of some kind, but could also possibly be caused by a headache, earache or toothache. It can be very difficult sometimes to identify the cause of a child's pain or resulting behaviour. A young child who has no communication problems will at an early age learn the word 'Ow!' and to point at where their pain is located. A child with autism and severe communication difficulties may have no means to let you know that something is hurting, and so the immediate cause of their behaviour is overlooked.

Sensory issues may cause a child to greatly dislike having their teeth brushed. This in turn can lead to tooth decay. Pain from toothache can be severe and if a child is unable to articulate that they have toothache, their behaviour may deteriorate.

Gut Problems: Constipation

Your child may have pain caused by a problem in their gut. Some gut symptoms may be noticeable even in a child who has no language or ability to communicate. Physical signs such as diarrhoea are very obvious. Bloating of the stomach or lower abdomen is easily visible. Constipation will be noticed earlier in a child who is not potty-trained as you will notice that they have not soiled their nappies. If your child is potty-trained and uses a toilet independently, you may not be aware that they are becoming constipated as they may not be able to tell you, and even if they could, they probably would not think that it is something that they need to tell you about. So, by the time you realize, the constipation may have been going on for a while. They may be in great discomfort, but unable to tell you.

Constipation may also be caused by a sensory issue and not just a physical one. It may be caused by a child resisting the need to pass solid waste. This could be due to a number of factors ranging from a fear of sitting on a toilet that is not familiar (for example, they may only defecate at home using their own toilet and refuse to use a toilet at nursery or school) to the fear of pain or discomfort when they actually pass a stool.

There could be many additional reasons. A child may, for an example, have an issue with the toilet seat being a different colour to that at home. The toilet may also be at a different height so they may feel uncomfortable sitting on it. There could be a sensory problem involving the room itself such as the smell or perhaps a dark room with no natural light, which may make them feel anxious in some way. There may be issues around embarrassment. Adults in hospital who are bed-bound often become constipated, partly from lack of movement or as a side-effect of medication, but one of the main causes is embarrassment at having to defecate in the presence of another person and to require the help of that person to wipe them afterwards.

If your child has had constipation in the past, defecating may have caused them pain at the time and so the memory of this pain may cause fear in the future. The problem then becomes a recurring one as they may try to resist the urge to defecate and try to hold onto it. Thus, the problem may begin as a sensory one and end up as a medical issue.

A child also needs to drink sufficient fluids throughout the day and some children do not like drinking very much and need encouragement just to drink an adequate amount. Again, sensory issues may be important here as a child may have very strict preferences as to what they will drink and from which cup or glass.

I am regularly asked for 'Winnie the Pooh juice', which is actually blackcurrant squash in a very old blue cup that many moons ago had a picture of Winnie the Pooh on it, now long since faded. I have to remember to show the cup to anyone else looking after my son as obviously there is no such cup in their eyes!

Impaction is a severe condition where a child is no longer able to defecate at all and so the gut becomes literally impacted or full of waste. This is obviously a very painful and potentially dangerous condition and needs careful medical management to overcome. There is no quick fix if your child ends up in this state and you must seek proper care from a doctor or hospital.

Sugar and Other Additives

For many children, not just those with autism, the removal of excess sugar in the diet is beneficial. Many manufactured foods have added sugar and other additives that can affect a child's behaviour. Some artificial colours are known to increase hyperactive behaviour. Any parent will have noticed that a young child going to a birthday party and being fed vast quantities of chocolate and other sweet items will return home in a hyperactive state. High levels of sugar are also found in foods that may be natural, e.g. fruit, and not just in manufactured and processed foods. Where possible, encourage your child to drink water and not large volumes of fruit juice or canned drinks. Check the packs of breakfast cereals as these too can contain high levels of sugar.

Sleep can be hugely affected by diet; a hyperactive child will find it very hard to settle and fall asleep. So trying to eliminate foods that contain excess sugar that may cause hyperactivity can help your child to sleep and, in turn, may reduce hyperactivity during the day as your child will not be permanently sleep-deprived and tired. Anyone suffering from lack of sleep or broken sleep will feel constantly tired – ask any parent with a newborn baby or a baby who is teething – but they may also feel almost manic at times due to extreme tiredness.

Many parents report beneficial changes and differences in their children when the levels of sugar in their diet are reduced, so this is definitely something worth trying with your child.

Stress

Owing to the high levels of stress created by having autism, many children suffer from physical problems caused by chronic stress. For our children with autism, the world can be a bewildering place with sensory overload in the form of constant noise, activity and visual input. Because they have a heightened response to everything around them, life can be overwhelming a great deal of the time.

I may be in a busy shopping centre or at a crowded event and begin to feel overwhelmed and crave some peace and quiet. I always leave at this point as, if I am feeling like this, my boys must be feeling very much worse. Over the years, I have tried to anticipate the point at which any of my boys will be suffering from sensory overload and try to leave before that point is reached. This can be a fine line sometimes as it usually means leaving while everyone else is still having a good time.

Along with the sensory overload, most children with autism find everyday life in general stressful. They may be anxious about things we cannot even guess at. If we are lucky, we may be able to identify some of those things and try to help to alleviate the anxiety as best as we can. Your child may be able to communicate their anxieties verbally, but if they cannot talk it can be very hard to pinpoint what may be causing them stress. Your child's own anxieties can range widely from a fear of inanimate objects, such as two different foods touching on a dinner plate, to a fear of social situations – and almost anything and everything in between. Your child may suffer from severe shyness or even a fear of people they do not know. Some children with autism also have a level of OCD, which, if severe, can shadow everything they do or experience. The need to line things up or sort things into categories such as colour is quite common in autism. If this order is not created, or allowed to be created, then your child may feel very stressed. Your child may be able to manage their world at home, but when not at home, the situation can be very different. Perhaps almost everything they do and everywhere they go may cause them some level of stress.

My boys have incredibly good memories for any past insult or perceived trauma. This means that they often carry a stressful memory with them when they re-visit a place or when they meet someone again.

So what effect does being constantly stressed have on the body? We know that in adults long-term stress can lead to nervous or physical breakdowns in some individuals. It can cause physical symptoms such as gut disturbances, headaches and the inability to sleep properly or relax. A constantly elevated heart rate or high-blood pressure can cause long-term damage to various organs of the body.

When we are stressed, the adrenal glands, which are situated in the kidneys, cause our bodies to produce additional adrenaline to help with the stress that the body is under. In a normal situation this is known as the 'flight or fight response' and is necessary to help the body to cope for short periods of extreme stress. It can cause a rapid heart rate and enable the person to keep functioning at an optimal level to help them get out of the situation that is causing them stress. In times of stress, such as exams or interviews or an accident, adrenaline will be produced. This is not necessarily a bad thing. People have been known to act heroically when under the influence of a high level of adrenaline. After the stressful situation is over, the person will often feel exhausted and need to rest. This is all part of normal functioning and is often necessary for human survival.

Ideally, stress should be eradicated from your child's world, but unfortunately with autism this is not going to happen. We can only take measures to alleviate some of the stress. For some children, this may be as extreme as removing them from school and perhaps educating them at home for a while. For others, it may mean trying to alternate stressful situations with periods of rest. This rest may not be purely physical, like sitting still or resting, but might mean a complete break from whatever is causing stress to your child.

Most children benefit from regular breaks from our over-stimulating modern world and this may simply mean connecting more with the natural world outside. Activities out in the open air, parks, beaches and the countryside all seem to calm our children, who benefit not only from the exercise, but from unpolluted air and an absence of unnatural noise and stimuli.

When my boys were still at a stage of running off and had to be held onto at any time they were out of the house, being out in an open space such as a park meant we all had more freedom. Although they might still run off, at least we did not have to forcibly hold their hands so it gave them some independence. It also meant that they were safe from traffic or other hazards, so we could all relax a little - even if relaxing meant running across an open space to retrieve them!

Epilepsy and Autism

There is still little understood or known about the connection between autism and epilepsy. Various studies show increased levels but an accepted figure seems to be that approximately one in four or 25 per cent of children with autism will have developed epilepsy by puberty. This is a very disturbing statistic, as epilepsy is a serious and frightening condition for any child to develop.

There are many different types of seizures or fits that can occur in a child with epilepsy, varying in severity from periods of absence previously known as *petit mal* to full-blown tonic-clonic seizures previously known as *grand mal* fits.

Absence Epilepsy or Petit Mal

If your child with autism is non-verbal and has periods where they appear to gaze into space and have no awareness of their surroundings, this may, in fact, be because they are having *absence seizures*. They may not have any physical symptoms so that they remain in the same position and have no shaking or trembling, but may appear temporarily vacant. They may be unresponsive to anyone or anything around them for a few seconds or minutes and appear totally unfocused. This can be a harder form of epilepsy to diagnose. It may be difficult to ascertain whether your child appears temporarily disconnected from their world because of their autism or because of a form of epilepsy. If you feel that absence epilepsy might be a possibility, you should seek advice from a doctor, who can carry out tests on your child.

Landau–Kleffner Syndrome

This condition was identified in 1957 by William Landau and Frank Kleffner. It can sometimes develop between the ages of eighteen months and three years, but most commonly occurs between the ages of three and seven. It is not included as part of the autistic spectrum, but may sometimes be misdiagnosed as autism. Its main symptom is gradual or sudden aphasia (language loss). So, in a child where the syndrome starts at a young age before language is acquired, it may be thought that the child has autism as they may have problems both speaking and understanding language. Where an older child who has developed normally and acquired language then starts to lose language, the possibility of this syndrome may be more obvious. Other symptoms include seizures. A small number of children have obvious seizures, but the majority have seizures during the night so these often go unnoticed. Such children may also be hyperactive and have a decreased attention span – again, symptoms that are often very similar to autism. The loss of language may occur over a long period of time, perhaps many months, so it may not be noticeable for a while.

A diagnosis is made by having EEG studies (electroencephalograms) of the brain carried out in a specialist hospital unit. Not many children with autism are offered EEGs, but if it is felt that your child had progressed normally for a while and then lost language, the possibility of this syndrome should be investigated.

Tonic-Clonic Seizures
Epilepsy often starts in the first three years of life, but some children with autism who have not had seizures beforehand do go ahead to develop epilepsy around puberty. These children may suffer from partial seizures or generalized tonic-clonic seizures.

Like autism, there is a spectrum in the severity of epilepsy, which is different in each child. There are varying types of seizure that may involve muscle stiffening alone, muscle stiffening along with jerky movements, sudden loss of tone or limpness, etc. The most serious and, unfortunately, the most common types of seizures or fits are those known as *tonic-clonic seizures* (*grand mal* fits). A child will stiffen and have jerky movements, fall to the ground and will lose consciousness. Again, the frequency or number of seizures varies from child to child.

A child having a seizure can be a frightening event for both the child and the carer. The child cannot control the seizure and prevent it from happening, although they may have some awareness that a seizure is on its way. If a child is non-verbal or has limited communication, then even if they get a feeling or a warning that a seizure is coming, they may not be able to tell anyone. The most important thing when a child is having a seizure is to keep them safe from danger and accidentally harming themselves. So if this happens to your child:

- keep calm
- move all objects out of reach (particularly heavy items

against which they may knock themselves accidentally)
- clear the immediate space around them
- hold their head slightly off the floor or place something soft like a coat beneath their head so they do not hurt their head during the fit
- if in bed, use a guard or cot-side on the side of their bed so they do not fall or roll out of the bed
- if at particular risk from head injuries due to falling, make sure they are wearing a helmet – your specialist should advise if any of these additional safety measures are necessary for your child.

All carers and those involved in looking after your child will need to have knowledge and training on how to keep your child safe during a seizure. Your child's carers need to know at what point they should summon medical help and call an ambulance (for example, if your child's fit lasts longer than a specified time). Staff within your child's school or nursery will also need to have adequate training. Some children may wear a medical alert bracelet or another form of identification so that information on their condition is readily available in an emergency. Emergency medication may need to be administered at the time in the form of a rectal suppository or medication placed within your child's mouth – how will your child's carers obtain this medication?

It is vital that your child has a diagnosis for epilepsy as soon as possible so that any treatment may commence. A child with suspected epilepsy will need to be referred to the care of a paediatric neurologist. A diagnosis may be made by various specialist tests, such as EEGs on the brain, which can be carried out while your child is awake or sometimes while they are asleep. In an active child with autism, performing some of these tests may not be easy and some children may require sedation in order for these to be carried out. Observation and record-keeping of any possible evidence of fits may also need to be kept, so sometimes the diagnosis can take a while.

There are various medications that can be prescribed to lessen the frequency or severity of the fits. As each child is an individual, sometimes it can be a long process to find the right drug at the right level for your child. It is not unusual for more than one drug to be prescribed on a regular basis. The drugs often need to be altered or tailored to your child as they grow as the drugs may become less effective with time. There may also be side-effects from the drugs, so trying to get the optimum levels to prevent fits occurring while also maintaining your child's everyday good health can be quite complex to balance. One of the most common side-effects is general tiredness and fatigue, often described as feeling 'groggy'. Your child may not be able to tell you other side-effects they may have that are causing them distress and increasing their difficult behaviours.

Some people believe that certain elements of a child's diet might trigger seizures, such as artificial colouring or preservatives, sweeteners or monosodium glutamate (MSG).

Diet
There is a great deal of dietary advice aimed at alleviating some of the symptoms of autism. Any actual link between diet and autism is, however, as yet unproven. For the time being, though, some parents report a difference in their child's behaviour after following specialist dietary interventions, such as removing gluten (found in wheat) from their child's diet. A gluten-free diet is the one most commonly associated with helping children with autism, so you may be recommended to trial the diet by other parents. A great deal of information on various dietary interventions and exclusions can be found online, but be aware that often it is not proven medical advice that you are reading. As with all advice on possible therapies, you need to be careful and to take informed advice on whatever you decide to try for your child. This may involve the assistance of a dietician or specialist clinic and should never be anything that may cause potential harm to your child. In the case of trying a gluten-free diet, for example, if you ensure that your child has adequate nutrition, then the worst the diet can possibly do is cost you additional expense and effort, but it should not harm your child.

Some of the basic dietary advice is relatively easy to follow, such as cutting down on foods containing artificial additives or extra sugar (*see* page 80). Other dietary interventions such as following a gluten- or casein-free diet can be more complex and much harder to follow. If you decide to try any of these diets, proper advice should be sought so that your child has the nutrition they require for bodily growth and for proper brain functioning.

4

SENSORY ISSUES

APART FROM FULFILLING SOME or several of the criteria within the diagnostic triad of impairments mentioned already in Chapter 1, there are many other additional problems that a child with autism may have. These may not form part of a formal diagnosis, but they do fit into the overall picture. These problems, or differences, usually come under the umbrella of a more loosely applied label, such as *sensory issues*. You may be told that your child has sensory issues, which can cover a myriad of different problems; some of these may seem to be fairly minor whereas there are others that can seriously affect your child's everyday existence and quality of life. The extent to which your child can be affected also varies enormously so that, for example, saying that your child has an issue with communication can vary from meaning your child is a non-verbal child who has no spoken language to one who has a normal range of language skills, but who struggles to hold a conversation.

What bothers one child may not bother another in the same way, even if their issues are the same. For example, your child may dislike an extreme of weather such as the cold. If you live in a warm climate, this will not be a particularly big issue unless you want to travel to another, colder country. If, however, you live in a colder climate, this may affect your child on a daily basis.

There are no definitive statements within the spectrum of autism that you can ever really make that will apply to all children universally. Outsiders may wish to categorize our children by saying that all children with autism seem to have certain dislikes or likes, but if you talk to parents, you will find that, like all human beings, every one of our children is unique and no two children are alike. However, there are some generalities within children on the autistic spectrum and so, while some will have certain issues, others may not, but they will usually have a combination of these issues to a greater or lesser extent.

Sensory Issues with Food

Possible Food Intolerances

You may notice that your child has red, burning hot ears sometimes, which can be a sign of food intolerance. In some children with autism, food intolerance is a serious medical issue and needs appropriate treatment. If you are concerned that your child may have a food intolerance, you should ask for a medical opinion. Intolerance to gluten, which is found in all wheat products such as bread, cakes and biscuits, may cause digestive problems and other symptoms if left unchecked.

Fussy Eating

Many children with autism are also selective eaters and can appear to be very fussy about which foods they will eat. They may be very limited in the variety of food that they will agree to eat due to several different factors. For example, the texture of meat can feel uncomfortable or strange in a child's mouth and they may dislike the sensation of chewing meat. Even the texture of minced meat may be disliked, despite the fact that it does not require much chewing. You may find that putting food into a blender helps as the texture is then broken down; this is a good way to encourage your child to eat more protein. You may have noticed that, as a baby, your child did not like it when you tried to introduce more lumpy foods and remove puréed food from their diet. They may have refused to eat it or even spat it out.

My boys all had enormous tonsils, which made swallowing food much harder for them. So for years we fed them puréed food. This ensured that they ate a balanced diet and grew well, but it proved harder later on when we tried to introduce more solid foods again. At the time, it meant that we didn't have to have battles with food and could concentrate on more important issues. I was concerned that their nutrition at an early age was important and so I decided to carry on with puréed food. However, this, of course, meant that their jaw and mouth muscles were not correctly exercised or stimulated, so this is not very helpful for a child with dyspraxia or who has speech delay. When we started to try and teach the boys to talk at around the age of three, we realized that we also needed to feed them solid foods. Sometimes, you have to weigh up the benefits of something against the negatives.

Of course, feeding your child puréed food is only practical when they are small. Later on you will still have to tackle the issue of trying to re-introduce solid food that needs chewing. You might need to experiment with different forms of protein to ensure your child's intake is sufficient. Eggs may be more easily swallowed in the form of scrambled eggs, and chicken is often more acceptable than beef to a child who dislikes the texture of meat. If your child will not eat solid foods, you may need to ask your GP to refer you to a specialist eating clinic and, in the meantime, your child may need supplementary milkshakes or protein drinks in order to keep up with their nutritional requirements.

Foods that have a strong smell or taste may also be refused. The sense of smell is very closely linked to taste and in children with autism smell can be a heightened sense. I tried to hide fish oil capsules in my boys' food and they soon became suspicious and started to sniff food before they would eat it. Ideally, your child should eat oily fish regularly, but in reality many children will refuse fish because of the smell, hence the fish oil capsules, many brands of which also smell. If you want to supplement your child's diet with fish oil capsules, then the expensive brands are more refined and tolerated better, some even come in flavoured chewy capsules to disguise their smell and taste.

Some children with autism will eat food of certain colours only or will perhaps refuse to eat foods of certain colours. Children may also only eat certain brands of food you give them on a regular basis and so eating away from home can be a problem. If you go to visit friends or relatives, it might be easier to explain and take your child's chosen brand with you. Familiar food is always comforting and a general dislike or suspicion of new things usually applies to food, too.

If you cut up your child's dinner when they wanted to eat it whole, such as cutting up fish fingers or cutting sandwiches into triangles and not squares, your child may have a tantrum and refuse to eat the cut-up food.

I always ask my children before I cut up any of their food. If someone else feeds them and they don't ask, but just go ahead and cut up the food, then there may be trouble and a hungry, cross child (and, sadly, perhaps a cross adult, too).

Some children will not eat different food together on the same plate, or they will refuse to eat if the food is touching another piece of food on the same plate. This can also apply to foods mixed together, like grated cheese on top of pasta, which you may need to serve on the side.

I had a child around for tea who wouldn't eat anything if it was touching another item on the plate. Fortunately, his mother had warned me beforehand.

Your child may only eat off a certain plate or drink milk from a particular glass. If this is the case, be prepared whenever you leave the house if you want to be sure your child will eat; take any necessary crockery with you. Although this may seem like you are indulging your child, this is something that needs to be worked on gently and slowly in your own home. Causing your child stress while away from home is never a good idea. Using cutlery can also be physically difficult for a child with motor delay or dyspraxia. It requires a certain amount of dexterity and coordination to be able to cut up food using both a knife and a fork at the same time. An OT may be able to help with this. To begin with, it is more important that your child eats in whatever way they can than how polite their table manners may be. You can work on these things later, but for now you want to engender a positive attitude towards eating and encourage your child and not worry about what other people might think or do. Your child's nutrition is the most important factor at this age, and encouraging healthy eating is much more important than manners or how your child actually eats.

Eating New Foods

Encouraging a small child to try something new to eat can be very difficult, and you will need lots of patience to achieve this (the same can be said for many other things in life, not just food). There may be occasions when you decide you have the time and energy to work on food issues with your child, but if you are concentrating on potty-training, for instance, you may wish to focus on that, instead. Choose which battles you are prepared to have at any time. You do not want food to become an issue and, if you feel that you are becoming stressed by your child's refusal to eat certain things, then there is a danger that you will pass that stress onto your child, and the whole eating problem can become a Catch-22 situation. In very severe cases, you may be able to get a referral to an eating clinic based in a hospital, which will be able to help you. Often, families will tolerate their child eating a limited diet so long as their food provides the nutrients that their child needs. If you are unsure whether your child's diet is sufficient, ask for a referral to a nutritionist. Your child requires food not just for their growth and energy, but also for their brain to work properly.

Sitting a Child Down to Eat

Initially, you may find that one serious problem with eating is keeping your child sitting down at the table long enough to eat. Your child may just be unable to sit still, and this is part of their autism. When your child is very little, you can feed them in a high-chair or a child's seat at the table with a harness and try to feed them as quickly as you can, with lots of distractions like singing or reading books. When your child is too big for a high-chair or toddler seat, then your problems can begin. It can be difficult enough in your own house persuading your child to sit and eat, but outside of the home in a restaurant or in someone else's house, it may become totally impractical as your child may get up and run around. Not only will other people judge your child's behaviour, but it can also be quite dangerous for your child to run around. Anywhere with an open door to the street can be hazardous. You will become stressed running after your child and no one will enjoy their meal. You may give up eating out in public for a long while until your child is able to sit and eat. One option for family outings might be a venue with a garden outside where everyone else's children may also be running around, or picnics, which tend to be much more relaxed. You may still need to choose a venue with an enclosed or fenced area as your child may run very quickly. It can be tiring as well as trying if you are constantly jumping up to run after your child to bring them back.

> I first noticed there was something different about my boys at a twins' first birthday picnic when all the other sets of twins stayed within reach of their mothers who were thus able to chat happily to each other and call their children to them without having to get up off the ground. Meanwhile, I was up and down constantly, running in different directions in an attempt to retrieve my two who appeared to ignore me calling their names. Certainly, they were not staying within range of everyone else. I wondered why my boys were so much harder to manage and, after that experience, decided picnics were not for us.

You can work at getting your child to sit at the table, but do not expect it to happen overnight. Having said that, you do not want to make food a constant topic for argument on a daily basis. Your child may just be a 'grazer' and prefer to eat on the run – literally! You might only be able to feed them small hand- or bite-sized pieces of food while they are otherwise distracted.

> I often hand-feed small pieces of sandwiches and fruit and biscuits to my youngest while he is sitting in the buggy with nothing else to do or while he is watching a DVD and he is almost unaware that he is eating at the same time.

Again, you may be judged as a lax parent if you allow your child to eat in front of the television, but if it works for you and your child, then you will just have to ignore the unwanted opinions of others. You will certainly not be judged by another mother with an ASD child, even if you are criticized by members of your own family.

> My boys all ate at a trio of coffee tables in front of the television for years as that was the only way I could distract them all to eat. I felt that we had had enough battles on our hands without having food battles, too, and keeping them healthy and well-fed seemed to be more important. No one can function at their best without adequate food and nourishment, so sometimes a compromise has to be reached.

Eating as a Social Activity

Family mealtimes may be hard; your child is expected to be able to sit and behave appropriately at the table, and they may not be able to do this. It is not their fault. In any case, behind closed doors, you should manage your child however works best for you and your family. In time, your child will learn to sit for short periods and eat, but they may never quite appreciate that for many adults mealtimes are a social occasion for conversation. As your child may not understand conversation or the need for it, eating for them is something that just needs to be done before you get on with something else. This aspect is particularly difficult for parents to explain to outsiders. If your child wants to eat and then leave the table, that may be fine at home but can be a hugely controversial issue for other wider family members who may be joining the dinner table. If it is hard not being able to eat out in restaurants as a family, it is harder still to have to refuse invitations from friends or family for meals. Even if your child's behaviour is tolerated, you may still find the social occasion too stressful as you will not be able to sit and enjoy your food or hold a conversation with anyone while you are occupied with looking after your child.

> We avoided open social occasions for many years with our boys and still only attend a few chosen events. Our boys need too much attention and are unable to conform to the behaviour many expect of them. Naturally, our focus is on them so we are unable to relax and enjoy ourselves.

Sensory Issues with Clothing

Sensory issues can vary, but a dislike of itchy clothing is very common. Some children are unable to tolerate seams and labels in clothes and it may take you a while to realize that is why they refuse to wear certain items. Online you can buy specialist clothing for children with sensory issues. You can buy vests, tee shirts, pyjamas and other clothing made without seams or labels. Some high street retailers also produce a limited range of school clothing, such as shirts, without labels in them. Tags and labels on clothing are often stitched on sensitive areas such as the neckline or at the waistband of trousers.

> If your child cannot tolerate labels, they will rip them out and leave holes in their clothing. Some of my boys' tops now have large holes at the neck where the label has been forcibly removed!

Natural fabrics like cotton tend to be much more comfortable to wear, with the exception of pure wool, which, although it is also a natural fabric, can also irritate. You may even find some pure cotton items are not as soft as others, often dependent on the price you pay.

Fleece is a useful modern fabric that is usually tolerated well and comfortable to wear. It also has the benefit of being easy to wash, and requires no ironing. It can get quite hot, though, and so is better for outer layers than those worn directly next to the skin. Sticky, plastic motifs and pictures on the front of pyjamas and tee shirts are also usually severely disliked by children with sensory issues. The plastic often creates a stiff, uncomfortable patch on the outside (and inside, too) of what would otherwise be a soft piece of clothing. Your child will probably pluck at the picture and try to pull it off. Embroidered motifs, appliquéd pictures or printed designs that are part of the fabric are usually much better tolerated. Generally, any clothing that has a cotton design on it should be comfortable against the skin.

For sleeping, your child will probably prefer 100 per cent cotton pyjamas, which again will be more expensive, but will hopefully be worn and not removed immediately after being put on! If necessary, remove the items from their packaging and feel how soft the cotton is, to be sure.

Bedding

Thread count is only measured in bedding such as sheets and duvet covers, and the higher the thread count is, the softer the cotton. You will probably want to choose 100 per cent cotton for bed-linen and avoid many of the fifty-fifty blends with polyester, which can be harsher against the skin and feel more scratchy. On the high street, most children's duvet cover sets decorated with popular characters from television and books are made from polyester blends for easy laundering. Although your child may really want a favourite TV character on their quilt cover, the fabric used may just be too itchy and uncomfortable for a good night's sleep. It also does not feel very good if it is hot and your child sweats in their sleep. There are children's sets made with 100 per cent cotton but you may need to search a little and avoid most of the cheaper high street shops.

Always wash everything first before your child wears it or sleeps in it to remove the chemicals used in the manufacturing process. These chemicals make the fabric harsher and stiffer and may also smell bad to your child, too. You may even need to wash some items a few times to make them softer.

School Uniform

Some mainstream manufacturers and high street shops now sell a limited range of school uniform items in natural fabrics for sensitive skins and some are made with softer seams and labels. Most high street shops sell cotton/polyester-mixed shirts, but a few do sell pure cotton ones. You will soon get used to reading clothing labels to check the fabric content. You may be able to adapt your child's school uniform with the agreement of the school if your child really cannot tolerate wearing certain clothing to ensure that your child's learning is not compromised by the fact that their clothing is irritating them all day. Some schools have their own uniforms printed with the school logo and these are often in synthetic mixes to make washing easier.

One of my sons takes off his school jumper whenever possible as he complains that it is itchy, but the jumper has the school logo on it, which means that it is the only option available.

If possible, though, you want your child to wear what their peer group is wearing so that they do not stand out from the crowd by wearing something different. If your child is starting a new school, you might want to get them used to wearing their uniform by getting them to practise wearing it at home for a while before they actually start school. That way their first day is not affected by any problems caused by wearing their uniform. However, your child may associate school uniform with actually going to school, in which case this would be counter-productive as you child might become confused and wonder why you are not taking them to school that day. This is another example of advice that might help one child but be confusing for another, and explains why there are no absolutes in caring for your child with autism. As with anything, gather all the advice you can and then adapt or choose whatever you think suits your child the best. If it does not work, bear in mind that there will always be different advice on offer.

Sensory Avoiding and Sensory Seeking

If your child is termed as *sensory avoiding*, they may try to allevi-ate the sensation that certain things apart from clothes can have on their skin. They may dislike the feel of the air or wind on their bare skin. They will almost certainly dislike the sensation caused by rain when it falls directly on their skin. Sometimes light rain can feel more 'painful' or uncomfortable on the skin than heavy rain.

If it rains unexpectedly, one of my boys will dive for cover by thrusting his head up and under my top as he cannot bear the sensation of rain on his bare skin. Nevertheless, he is happy to go swimming or to have a bath because the water is much 'heavier' in those circumstances.

If your child is very sensitive to the elements, they may prefer to wear long-sleeved tee shirts and long trousers and avoid shorts and tee shirts as this will lessen the sensations felt. This could make them very hot and uncomfortable in very warm weather, so they may need loose clothing such as long-sleeved shirts and baggy trousers. Again, school uniform could be a problem as most PE kits include shorts and tee shirts. Your child may prefer to wear tracksuit bottoms as an alternative. A hat is also a good idea in the winter months to keep the wind out of their ears or from blowing through their hair. If you have a young child, their intolerance to the elements will be particularly noticeable when they are on a swing or at the playground on a rapidly moving piece of equipment that causes a strong current of air. The feel of the wind on their skin can be very uncomfortable for them. Try putting a hat and gloves on your child even if you do not think it is particularly cold outside. Your child may be much happier.

Children with sensory issues often prefer thick socks and solid shoes to pad the nerve endings on their feet. As your child may not like to be barefoot, it may help if they wear slippers around the house or slipper socks with reinforced soles. Your child may actively dislike walking on sand and the first time you take your small child to the beach, they may lift their feet up immediately when you put them in contact with the sand. Beach shoes such as cotton sandals, rubber shoes or waterproof activity shoes may all help. Sand can be a huge irritant to many children and adults, not just those with autism. Many adults dislike the feel of sand even if they have no obvious traits of autism. Although children with ASD generally like to play with sand, the sensation of dry sand stuck between toes or within clothing can be horribly uncomfortable and ideally you should shower your child to rinse off all the sand as soon as you can, especially if you have a long car journey home. If your child has been swimming in the sea, you should also shower and rinse the salt off as soon as possible as dried salt on the skin can be itchy and irritating, too. Those towelling, hooded beach cover-ups can be really useful as they instantly alleviate the feel of the air on damp skin and are heavy and comforting to a child with sensory issues. You can buy them to fit children up to teenage sizes and may even be able to find one in an adult size. A hooded towel or poncho-style towel can also be useful.

If, however, your child is termed as sensory seeking, they may actively seek out the sensations that the sensory-avoiding child avoids. So, your child may only want to wear shorts whatever the weather and will take off their shoes and socks at any opportunity in order to be able to feel the sensation of the ground. They will enjoy being wrapped in a blanket tightly and the sensation of heavy pressure, like hugging. There are padded or weighted items of clothing, such as vests, available that help some children with severe sensory issues. An occupational therapist may advise on the wearing of these.

Of my twins, one is sensory avoiding and the other sensory seeking, so they have always worn very different clothing. While one would live all year round in shorts, the other would happily wear long trousers whatever the weather. Like all things, though, this has lessened with time and patience, and now both happily wear the appropriate clothing for the season. However, one still prefers to wear thin socks while the other will only wear thick socks, ideally with extra padded soles.

Practical Difficulties with Clothing due to Poor Motor Skills

Many children with autism tend to find buttons, zips and getting dressed much harder than other children of a similar age. This may be due to a level of dyspraxia or poor fine motor skills. It may be tempting to keep your child in tracksuit bottoms for ease, but you also need to consider that, ideally, your child should not stand out from their peers and at some stage they will need to wear normal clothing. If you are doing potty or toilet training, try to get clothes with elasticated waistbands for your child to wear so that they can be as independent as possible. Most school clothes have elasticated waistbands up to quite large sizes and it is possible to find older children's clothes without zips and buttons. Obviously sportswear tends to have fewer fastenings, but if you want ordinary clothes you can still search around and find things without zips. Some of the online children's wear companies have clothes in larger sizes in natural fabrics with elasticated waists or those with adjustable waistbands with internally placed buttons, so you do not need to fit an exact size that way. It is also more comfortable for an active child to wear clothes with some give and stretch in them. Those such as jeans with metal fastenings around the waistband and zips can dig in a child's skin and irritate, so avoid.

Difficulties with Shoes

Putting on shoes and tying shoelaces can be very hard for some children. Many children with autism have a degree of dyspraxia or poor fine motor skills. Try to avoid younger children's shoes with buckles as you or someone else will constantly have to help your child to get their shoes on and off. It is fairly easy to find shoes in children's sizes with Velcro fastenings to avoid laces. Many makes of school shoes, and even gym shoes or pumps, are now made with Velcro fastenings. If your child cannot do up laces unaided, this can make them stand out from other children – particularly if they have to ask an adult to help them after a certain age when the rest of their peer group can manage alone. There are even some adult shoes now made with Velcro fastenings.

For older children and teenagers who have grown out of children's sizes, you can now get laces with a click part like a toggle, which they pull together to tighten the laces. There are some laces available for special needs and elderly people online or from special needs companies. Recently, sports companies have produced elastic laces with toggle fastenings for specialist sports like triathlon where the runners need to make a speedy change of shoes and do not have time to stop and tighten laces. These are easily available online and can be substituted for ordinary laces in trainers. These laces are a cheap and very practical solution. There are also elastic twisty laces that do not require knotting, but they may need a certain level of dexterity to pull tight enough. Wellington boots are obviously easy to put on unaided, but often require a great deal of pulling to remove – even for adults! Wellies have a tendency to be cold and damp, though, so your child may be miserable in cold weather if their feet are cold. Boot socks may help or a more expensive alternative are outdoor shoes or boots made with Gortex or a similar waterproof material.

My boys all wore waterproof leather shoes or short boots in the winter. They doubled as school shoes and removed the need for wellies. Although they were more expensive, it meant that the boys were able to jump in puddles on the way to school and not be uncomfortable as their feet stayed warm and dry all day.

Many children like their comfortable, old worn-in shoes and dislike new, stiff ones. For some children just having to try on and wear new shoes can be a source of great trauma. This is probably due to the discomfort and stiffness that new shoes have until they have been broken in. The problem is that children's feet grow so quickly that you have no option but to buy them new shoes fairly often.

My boys used to go into total meltdown in shoe shops having to try on new shoes. We would try and buy shoes only when there was no one else in the shop and find a sympathetic shop assistant! We would then have to hide their old shoes and tolerate tantrums for days when putting on the new shoes. We would find a very reinforcing activity that they really wanted to go to and whisk them straight out of the house in order to take their attention away from the shoes.

You can buy a foot measure to use at home to measure your children's feet. This will at least mean that you can save unnecessary trips to the shoe shop if their feet have not grown. It also means that you can buy shoes online if shoe shops are really too difficult to manage while your child is quite young. Hopefully, like many other problems, this will ease in time and there may come a time in the future when your child is actually eager for new shoes and bowing to peer pressure to have a particular brand of shoe or type.

Sensory Issues Linked to Cleaning and Grooming

Brushing and Cutting a Child's Hair

Hair combing and cutting can cause enormous distress to a child with sensory issues. It can actually cause pain to a child when you try to comb or cut their hair because of their heightened sensitivity. You can avoid brushing and combing most children's hair most of the time except when they reach school age and you get the dreaded 'nit letter' and are forced into serious time-consuming combing. A metal specialist nit comb is the only option if your child gets nits as the plastic combs scratch horribly.

Sometimes using a de-tangle spray or conditioner after washing hair can help with combing or brushing hair while wet. It may also be beneficial before a haircut.

I still only really brush my boys' hair after a bath or occasionally they will allow me a few well-aimed swipes as they walk out of the door in the morning.

Having a haircut can be a major trauma to a child with autism due usually to an over-sensitivity to one or more factors. Your child may be fearful of the buzzing and vibration of the clippers, so it may be better to cut with scissors only. They may dislike the feel of the hair dropping onto their shoulders so you could try wrapping them in a towel to keep the cut hairs off their skin. You should be prepared for a speedy change of clothing after a haircut as hair can stick to fabric easily and cause discomfort. Hairdressers usually have a big soft brush to keep removing any stray hairs as they fall. If you are cutting your child's hair at home, this might be something you could consider buying. There is also an unpredictability about having your hair cut, the hairdresser needs to talk to your child throughout and tell them which bit they are going to cut as they go to avoid unpleasant surprises. It may help for your child to be seated in front of a mirror to watch what is happening. You could try and distract them with a favourite toy. An older child may be happy to play with a hand-held gaming device and, likewise, a younger child could be distracted with a book. This will be a good case scenario, though, as many children seem to have an almost pathological fear of having their hair cut, and will scream so much that the game or book may not even be noticed. You may need to snip at their hair in tiny stages so that you cut a few bits at a time and your child learns to trust you so that each time they tolerate a bit more.

I snip for days cutting a little bit at a time on my youngest while he watches a video. It's not perfect but it saves a lot of upset.

A verbal child may be able to tell you what it is that they particularly dislike so that you can find a solution, but many very young children with autism will not have the language or the means to communicate their worries and fears to you. Some mothers even resort to trying to cut their child's hair while they are asleep. Others will have their child's hair cut very short so that they can have a longer interval between cuts. You may find that your child dislikes having short hair as their hair can protect their heads from wind and rain.

One of my sons who can now talk says he likes his hair to cover his ears as he feels the cold. One of my other sons likes his hair short as he hates the feel of a fringe of hair on his face. So we have two different children wanting the opposite thing to each other and before they could talk we had no idea of this. Once again, this emphasizes that each child has different issues and the hard task for you is to try to work out what is right for your child.

Sadly, difficulties with hair cutting is a very common problem and if you search online you will find many other suggestions and ideas of how to help your child get through a haircut. You may find yourself learning how to cut your own child's hair to avoid having to take them to a strange place where their screams will not be appreciated. You might be able to find a freelance hairdresser who is willing to come to the house and take time to cut or is prepared to leave and return another day if necessary. Unless your child is cooperative, a hairdresser's or barber's shop is not a good idea. Some children will tolerate clippers, which makes the job much easier and safer as you do not have sharp scissors involved, but many will dislike the vibration and sound the clippers make. If your child needs to have their hair washed at the hairdressers, you could take your own shampoo as the strong scent of an unfamiliar shampoo may be distressing. Ideally, just wetting your child's hair should be enough as the whole process of washing hair in an unfamiliar place with your head tipped backwards is not comfortable and water can go down the back of your neck, which may be enough to upset your child before you even start the actual haircut. Some people resort to very short haircuts for their children so that they do not have the additional problems of combing or brushing to deal with. Your child is not being naughty when they scream, they may feel great discomfort and fear when someone tries to cut their hair and it is one of those things that they will slowly start to tolerate over time.

One day you will be sitting in the hairdresser's while your child is getting a proper haircut without any real fuss and you will remember the days when they screamed and screamed and it will seem almost like you must have imagined it. My boys had to have their hair cut at home for years as they screamed and tried to run away. They now sit and tolerate a haircut at the hairdresser's although we have never been tempted to add hair-washing to the procedure yet.

Dental Care

Your child may find brushing their teeth an uncomfortable experience, too – again, for sensory reasons. Try to find a soft toothbrush as your child may have very sensitive teeth and gums. You may need to experiment with different brands of toothpaste as some have a very strong flavour and may add to the reasons why your child will not let you brush their teeth. A children's electric toothbrush may help some, but others might not be able to tolerate the buzzing noise. A younger child's toothbrush may still be more suitable for an older child as it will be smaller and softer. Your child may find it more comfortable to brush their own teeth than when you do it for them; this is because they can control where the brushing is, so try to get them doing it independently as early as possible. You should also talk while you do it and tell them which area you are going to brush as you do it. Imagine if you were at the dentist and having the right side of your mouth treated, and suddenly you were poked in the left side with no warning – you, too, would jump.

If you are unable to brush your child's teeth, cavities and holes can form easily and can cause great distress and real discomfort and pain. If your child does develop holes in their teeth that require filling, they may need a general anaesthetic in order for this to be carried out. Not many children with ASD will safely tolerate a dentist filling their teeth in the normal manner, i.e. in the dentist's chair. A general anaesthetic will entail going to hospital and all the issues surrounding a hospital admission, including the anaesthetic and any needles involved. There will probably be a long waiting list even to get it done. So aim for prevention. It is much more important that you manage to brush your child's teeth than that you manage to brush their hair.

Personal Hygiene

Personal hygiene and bathing can sometimes become a problem. Again, children like the familiar and you may find your child will refuse to get into a bath that is not their own.

On holiday, one of my sons refused to use the bath in the holiday house. The next year, we stayed near the seaside and I needed to at least rinse the sand and salt off him. In the end, the only way I could get him into the bath was by getting in myself and having him passed to me to sit on my lap while I very quickly washed him.

Your child might have a memory of slipping and be fearful of that, so a non-slip mat in the bottom of the bath is a good idea. When washing their hair in the bath, a shower attachment is often too harsh because of the noise it makes and the effect of 'prickly' water, which is not gentle. It is kinder to wash hair using a cup of water poured over your child's head. Again, they may have a memory of perhaps getting shampoo in their eyes and will then retain a fear or dislike of the bath and having their hair washed. For many children, a bath-time routine is a good idea to calm them before they go to bed, but if you attempt to put them in the bath at a different time of day – perhaps because they are covered in mud – they will probably refuse because it is out of their usual routine to bath at a different time of day. Your child might tolerate a shower if they can shower with another person, for example, showering with Daddy as a treat. Be aware that the water temperature in a shower can change very fast and if your child gets scalded by the water being too hot, or the water suddenly becomes too cold, this may upset them and put them off having a shower again. At least, if they shower with an adult, you can swiftly remove them or change the water temperature. If they do develop a fear of the bath, you may need to take it in very small stages to get them used to it again, perhaps by just dipping a hand or foot in for a few days, then maybe just standing in the bath for a few days before finally sitting down again in a full bath. A caring sibling to play with them in the bath might also reassure them. Be careful of what you add to the bath water in the form of bubble bath as the smell might be too strong or the additives may cause itching, so use soap-free bubble bath or non-allergenic versions. Most children enjoy a bath even if they dislike rain or being accidentally splashed by water.

Issues with Sleep

Not all children with autism have sleeping issues, so it is not listed as one of the areas included in diagnosis. However, problems with sleep are very common in children with ASD. Nearly all parents will experience some sort of sleeping problem in their child at some stage in their development.

Your child may have problems getting to sleep, staying asleep or may not appear to need very much sleep at all. All of these can cause your child to have insufficient sleep overall and will impact on their lives, not to mention the other family members whose lives will also be affected by your child's sleep issues. Mothers with newborn babies somehow manage to keep going with little sleep due to their baby waking during the night for feeds. It is thought that the hormones produced after giving birth and during breast-feeding help a little with the lack of sleep a new mother gets. However, this is usually a short-term problem as the baby matures and learns to sleep through the night within a short period of time, or a little longer in some cases. A child with autism may never manage to sleep through the night and for those mothers, the strain of long-term lack of sleep can be severe. Sleep problems are also known to be more common in children with autism than in most other developmental disorders, although it is not really known why this is.

Sleep Deprivation in Parents

For the child who does not get enough sleep, they too will be stressed and tired during the day. Inevitably, this will impact on their behaviour, their attention span, general mood, appetite and almost every part of their daily living. It is therefore not just a problem with sleeping, but a problem that has an impact on everything else in your child's life. The combination of parents and children with constant lack of sleep can be very debilitating for the whole family. Unfortunately, it is often the children with a more severe learning difficulty who seem to suffer the most from sleeping problems, and their parents are probably the ones who are most exhausted and need their sleep. It can even impact on your married life and relationship if one of you has to be awake for half of the night and is then tired and irritable during the day. You may end up almost having to take shifts between you so that you can at least get the minimum sleep necessary. A child who has interrupted sleep cannot share a room with a sibling as their brother or sister would also then suffer from lack of sleep.

Some children with ASD are hyperactive, either physically or mentally or both. This will often mean that they have difficulty in getting to sleep as they cannot wind down at the end of the day. A very stressed child may also have a problem falling asleep in the same way that adults under severe stress cannot relax and fall asleep easily. Nearly all children with ASD are stressed in some way, either by their environment or in a sensory way; just trying to live and function in a world that is not suited to them can be hugely stressful. At the end of a long, physically and mentally draining day, you may be longing to get to bed and switch off, but your child is still fully awake and rushing around and refusing or unable to go to sleep. You cannot go to bed as your child needs watching at all times. So how do you cope?

Having had a baby with severe colic and having endured sleepless nights for years, I sympathize enormously with parents of children who never get into a proper sleep routine.

Sleep deprivation can be more detrimental to health than the lack of food. In adults, sleep deprivation can cause problems with attention and decreased cognitive skills. Fatal accidents have been caused by tired drivers nodding off at the wheel on long car journeys. There are numerous other results of a lack of sleep that significantly impede daily life. So trying to address your child's sleep problems is as important for you as it is for your child.

Learning to sleep is a developmental stage. In neurotypical children, there is a known sleep pattern that develops with age and maturity. This does, of course, vary between children and can be influenced by factors such as breast-fed babies feeding more frequently during the night than babies fed on formula, and larger birthweight babies sleeping longer during the night as they can take larger feeds. The routines and patterns that the rest of the household follow can also be adjusted. Sometimes working parents may wish their young children to go to bed at a later time so they can spend time with them in the evenings, whereas a mother at home may need that break to herself at the end of the day and be happier for an earlier morning start. By the age of four, most children will be in an acceptable sleep routine, which means that they will sleep through the night for a set amount of hours.

The sleep-wake cycle is a circadian rhythm dependent on light and darkness. In some children with autism, this seems to be interrupted for some reason and so the child may wake up during the night, perhaps at 2 a.m. or 3 a.m. while it is still dark. They will be fully awake and unable to go back to sleep for the rest of the night, or for at least a few hours. Whether this is caused by something physical, is a developmental problem, or down to behaviour is not entirely known. It may have different causes in different children. Obviously, if your child is awake like this during the night, an adult also needs to be awake with them. This adult is often someone who cannot catch up on sleep during the day, and so suffers from continual sleep deprivation.

Having difficulties getting to sleep may be caused by your child being anxious or stressed. They may be afraid to be in bed on their own and need someone with them until they fall asleep. Your child may need a night light for reassurance.

My children all have blackout linings on their curtains, which certainly helps to minimize daylight waking them up early in the summer months.

Try to make your child feel that their bedroom is a safe environment for them. This may mean painting the walls a plain light colour or perhaps choosing a very bright quilt cover if this has your child's favourite story character on it. This will be a very individual issue, so it may take some trial and error to get right. Do remember that change may be hard for your child to cope with, so try not to keep changing things around. Most children naturally adopt a favourite bear or toy to carry around as infants, which can be comforting. Some children with ASD never seem to do this, but may form an attachment to a soft toy later on. This seems to be another developmental stage that can occur later than with neurotypical children. You can try to enhance this by offering the same toy at night to give a hug, too, or perhaps choosing a toy that ties in with a favourite game or bedtime story such as the Gruffalo, or pyjamas with Thomas the Tank Engine on them.

Resolving Sensory Issues Affecting Sleep

Are sensory issues affecting your child's sleep? Are they being irritated by their pyjamas having seams or being made from a 'scratchy' fabric? Have you made their bed using sheets or quilt covers made of synthetic fabric that may irritate your child's skin? Your child may need a heavyweight quilt to reduce sensory over-load. If they are very restless and kick the bedclothes off while sleeping, they may need to wear a sleepsuit or 'onesie' over their pyjamas with just a light cover, instead, to help prevent them from waking up because they are cold. If their bedroom is near a noisy street, the traffic noise may be keeping them awake or a street light may be causing too much light and disturbing them. It could also be that their bedroom is too hot or too cold or that there is a draught coming from a window. If you have heating left on overnight, this can make the air very dry and the room stuffy, so you might try a humidifier in the room to add moisture to the air. Try to address any sensory or physical problems with your child's bedroom before you start any behavioural approach to sleep. A guard on the side of the bed may help your child to feel more secure and remove any concern that they might fall out of bed. You can buy softer travel forms of these so that your child will not wake up if they bump into the edge and so that you can use them on any bed your child may sleep in.

Another major cause of sleep problems may be your child

being in discomfort or pain, for example, from a bloated tummy or constipation. They may have earache or toothache. Lying down will worsen the pain as will the fact that they have nothing else to distract them from it (if you are busy, it is possible to ignore a niggling ache, but when you have nothing else to concentrate on, then the ache magnifies). Try to eliminate any possible physical causes: if you are not sure if your child has any stomach problems, get advice from a doctor. It will be fairly obvious if your child has constipation (*see* page 79) and this will cause enough discomfort to affect their sleep.

Keeping a Sleep Diary

You may want to start by keeping a form of sleep diary so that you note down at what time your child finally went to sleep and anything you had to do to aid this, such as staying in the room, what and when they last ate or drank, whether they had a good or bad day preceding going to bed, or if there was any obvious cause of stress or discomfort.

If your child wakes during the night, you should note down at what times they woke and then went back to sleep and whether you had to do anything to get them to sleep again and how they behaved during that wakeful period (e.g. if they were drowsy or agitated). Finally, note at what time they woke in the morning and what their mood was like on waking. After a while you may see a pattern and this will help any experts you consult who may be able to offer you advice on how to break these patterns.

Encouraging a Sleep Routine

There are various things you can try to help establish a sleep routine, similar to those used to teach a baby or toddler how to sleep. A very regular routine can help enormously, such as putting your child to bed at the same time each day, preceded by a warm bath and a bedtime story.

If you have an older child who can follow a story, then story tapes might be useful. Although my boys are much older now and are able to talk, they will never be able to follow a story read on a tape or read a story themselves for pleasure or relaxation. This may be due to a number of reasons. For one, a tape will only read at a set pace, which may be too fast for your child to follow. Reading a story aloud to your child means that you can tailor your reading to suit your child, pausing to check that they have understood certain words; reading more slowly and with more appropriate emphasis, if required. Reading may indeed simply be a mechanical skill in which your child can decipher actual words, but never really understand the meaning of them or what a story is trying to convey. Reading and digesting facts is very different to understanding the hidden messages contained within a story.

Avoid electronic devices at bedtime like computers or hand-held devices, as these tend to stimulate the brain and will keep your child 'wired' so that they will be unable to relax and go to sleep. Similarly, try not to have a television or DVD player in your child's bedroom. Music and gently rocking your child may soothe them, but you need to try to avoid the habit of getting into bed with your child and staying with them until they fall asleep. They may need the reassurance that you are near, so you can start by checking on them at regular short intervals, which you can gradually lengthen. There are social stories for older children that you can use to talk through with your child to find out if something is causing them anxiety about the process of sleeping. Some children with ASD additionally have ADHD or ADD, which can make it harder for them to relax and fall asleep naturally. They may also need less sleep than you, unfortunately!

One of my sons, who also has ADHD, cannot settle at night and we often end up with him on the sofa with us until we go to bed. It is not ideal, but for a child who cannot read and is too old to play, it is more relaxing and conducive to sleep for him than the alternative, which is to allow him to play on a computer before bed-time.

You may need advice from a special needs health visitor or other therapist to formulate an individualized programme for your child to help with any sleep issues. This will probably be in the form of a behaviour plan once you have eliminated any underlying sensory or medical problems.

Sensory Issues with Toilet Training
This is another important area of your child's development. Firstly, before you even think about tackling potty-training, you need to

sort out any bowel issues your child may have. You will not be able to successfully potty-train a child with gut issues (*see* page 79) if they are unable to control their own bowel movements.

One of my sons had diarrhoea on and off until the age of three. I knew I would not be able to potty-train him because of it. A friend helped me to identify that eating bananas was causing it. He had been intolerant to all fruit from birth but, even though we had avoided the more obvious citrus fruits, we had presumed bananas would be fine to introduce to him as he grew older. As soon as we realized that they were a problem, we removed bananas from his diet. That stopped the diarrhoea, and I was able to begin potty-training him.

It is harder to potty-train a child who is non-verbal than a child who is able to talk and can communicate easily with you. Many people delay potty-training a child with ASD as they see it as a momentous undertaking.

A friend I met in the early days had potty-trained his non-verbal son at just three and said how much of a feeling of achievement it gave him and his child in the midst of so many other problems. This was one success and gave him hope.

It is very possible to toilet train a non-verbal child, so do not put it off and wait until your child is verbal. It is also a physiological stage of development and most children with ASD follow a similar developmental path to other neurotypical children with sitting, walking and other milestones, although they may be slightly delayed in one area or another but usually within the limits set for normal development.

Potty-training will be harder if your child does not have much or any language skills. However, success is still achievable. I potty-trained all my boys at a young age while they were basically still non-verbal.

If your child is over the age of three and still in nappies, you should be able to get nappies supplied by the NHS through your health visitor. Your health visitor should also be able to supply you with other continence aids, such as special pants for older children.

Wearing nappies can be a sign to other children that your child has a problem and could put your child at risk of bullying.

> I started to potty-train my boys as soon as I knew they were starting nursery as I didn't want them to stand out from the other children or be different.

By the time your child starts school, nearly all the other children will be toilet-trained, even if they are not yet dry overnight. If your child will be going to a mainstream school, ideally they should be toilet-trained before they start. It will not be noticed if they need some help with going to the toilet, but wearing a nappy will be very obvious to the other children. Also, your child may begin to feel 'different' if they are not using the toilet like everyone else.

> Because I started toilet-training after the age of three, my boys were all big enough to use a full-sized toilet. This seemed to make more sense to me than using a tiny child's potty on the floor. As I was unable to explain anything verbally, my boys had to learn by example, so using a normal toilet was the obvious thing to do.

Your child will have spent most of their life accompanying you to the toilet or following you in there, so they should be aware of what you use a toilet for. If you have older siblings, they may also have observed them using a toilet, so producing a small plastic potty may not make visual sense to your child. There are also small potties that fit into a seat with arms and a base: these are more stable and stand on the ground. They resemble a toilet and the top can also be lifted off and placed on an adult toilet so that you can train your child in stages. If you have a very small child who is able to understand simple words such as 'wee', you may be able to use a child's potty, but most parents leave potty-training until their child is a bit older.

There are many different issues around potty-training. Your child may not want to use the toilet if they have constipation as they will associate the toilet with pain. They may be fearful of falling into the water below. They may feel unstable as their feet are not on the ground (a toilet step may help with this). Some children will only use a toilet that they are familiar with.

> I know a teacher who covered a school toilet seat in black tape as the child would only use a toilet with a black seat as that was what she had at home.

A child with any sort of OCD issues will be easier to train if they really dislike the sensation of being wet.

> One of my twins hated being wet or dirty and was potty-trained within days while his twin brother was not bothered at all and took over a year to toilet-train successfully!

There are often behavioural issues around toilet-training. Some of these you can take advantage of. For example, some boys will find the action of peeing into a toilet very reinforcing, so try putting a cork into the toilet bowl: the cork will tend not flush away and it will give your son something to aim at! Many children find it more comfortable to poo into a nappy than to sit on the toilet so this may be difficult to overcome. To begin potty-training, you might want to start in the way that all parents start, which is to regularly offer your child the chance to 'wee' or 'poo'. You might start slowly by sitting your child on the toilet at obvious times, such as after eating food or just before a bath, and then increase this every thirty minutes or so. Many children will urinate as soon as you stand them in the bath, so be ready to pick them out quickly and put them on the toilet so that you catch a little in the right place. You can then reward your child enormously. Part of the behavioural side of potty-training is to praise your child for any action in the potty or on the toilet, while refraining from any negative comments if your child has an accident. You can start by praising your child just for sitting for any length of time. It may be a while before your child perhaps does urinate in the right place and can start to associate the action with the toilet or potty. If your child has an accident or urinates in the wrong place, try not to react at all: children are rewarded by negative reinforcement almost as much as by positive reinforcement. For some children, any reaction from you, whether good or bad, can be rewarding and can encourage attention-seeking behaviour. This attention-seeking behaviour can then escalate to the point where your child is deliberately doing something you disapprove of simply in order to gain your attention. With an older child, you might be able to use some form of chart with rewards and stickers for every appropriate action in the toilet. Verbal praise may be enough for some children, but others may require instant rewards, perhaps in the form of being allowed to watch a DVD or a small snack. Tailor your actions to your child.

You may need to stay in the house for the first week or so of potty-training, so be prepared beforehand with lots of activities to keep you and your child from becoming bored. You may wish to start off by removing your child's nappy completely and putting them on the potty or toilet at regular intervals. Every time they start to urinate, you will need to be able to stick them straight onto the toilet, so you may need to stay in the part of the house nearest to the toilet. This may sound obvious, but if your only toilet is located upstairs and you are downstairs playing, you will never get your child upstairs in time! You might want to try pants instead of leaving your child bare. People often leave potty-training until the warmer months so that they can leave their child without trousers on. You will certainly need trousers that pull up and down very easily if your child needs to wear them; dungarees are the worst possible item for potty-training! Buy cheap pants from big supermarket chains. If you are out of the house and your child does a poo, you can just throw the pants away; they can often be cheaper than the larger-sized nappies. It is quite difficult to potty-train a child who is still wearing nappies as they do not get the sensation of feeling wet and it is hard to notice when they are urinating. In fact, they may not even notice themselves.

Other Sensory Issues

Another sensory issue may be that your child likes the texture of things like glue and mud on their hands.

One of my boys constantly made mud in the garden in a big hole created with water from the hosepipe. Eventually, we had to get a removable tap-head for the outside tap to stop him doing it. He would bury small toy people and other objects in the mud, some of which emerged only years later.

You may be able to redirect your child to play with more appropriate material like play dough, although some children may also try to eat play dough, which contains gluten. You can find recipes online for home-made dough that will not cause problems if eaten! An OT may also be able to advise on more appropriate items for your child to squeeze or play with, such as specialist putty.

Unfortunately, this desire for squeezing and playing with a malleable substance can lead your child to play with their own faeces. This is a very unpleasant activity for all concerned and one that can be quite difficult to eradicate. Your child may smear or spread poo around their bedroom, on walls and floors, and on their own bodies. This is one of the distressing aspects of autism – and quite a demoralizing one, too.

The same son who played with mud also smeared poo, and I remember one day walking in to find poo everywhere. He was covered in it and so too was the hall floor. There was so much poo around that I didn't know whether first to clean up my son or the poo in which my youngest child was about to crawl!

Even worse, of course, is if your child does this while you are visiting someone else's house – it's a highly effective way to find out just how tolerant your friends are! Again, this is a phase and children do grow out of it eventually. If you search online, you will find ideas and tips from others on how to cope with this particular activity. One such suggestion is to use sleepsuits to prevent your child access to the contents of their nappy.

If I tell people that my talking, almost self-caring teenager used to play with his own poo, they wouldn't believe me now. I can hardly believe it myself. Although it may seem like it will never be resolved, have faith that it will.

Noise Sensitivity

Some children are very sensitive to noise. You may find your child is frightened of certain noises at home, like the vacuum cleaner or hairdryer, and be particularly sensitive to sudden, unexpected noises. Letting them push the vacuum cleaner and taking control of the noise may help. Home renovation that entails loud banging, drilling and electrical noises can be hugely alarming for a child who is sensitive to noise. Large sports halls often have an echo that may cause distress and you may first notice this when your child is invited to a birthday party in a big school hall. Of course, their distress could be because they are anxious in a new environment, but equally it could be the echoey noise they cannot tolerate. In the same way, big shopping malls and airports can be overwhelming because of the sounds being bounced back all around on top of the additional sensory overload caused by all the people and lights and colours in the building. Whenever you start to feel that a place is just too much and you need to get home for some peace and quiet, your child will probably have felt like that from the moment you arrived. Some parents find that ear-defenders can help with this problem. However, in the long run, you need to try to desensitize your child, if possible, as walking around wearing a pair of ear-defenders will tend to draw attention to your child. Some children, while not tolerating the noise that other children make, will have no problem making their own very loud noise! This may be because the noise they make is under their own control and they can anticipate it.

Cinemas can be difficult places for children with autism. Not only do they need to sit still and concentrate, they also need to be able to tolerate the loudness of the soundtrack and lighting levels that may be quite dim. The cinema can be an overwhelming sensory environment for any child with autism. Some cinemas now run occasional autism-friendly screenings where the sound is turned down, the lights are on low and – the best bit of all – all the other parents attending are in the same position as you. If your child gets up and down, cannot sit still but runs around and shouts out, you are not glared at by people who do not understand. This is ideal while you are getting your child adjusted to new situations.

Our boys all attended autism-friendly screenings for years until they were able to sit happily and watch all the way through a film with no problems at all. They still dislike sitting too near the screen and in contrast to neurotypical children, they don't like 3D films at all as the visual overload is too much for them.

Over-Stimulating Environments

School environments can be over-stimulating for a child. Although teachers will try to maintain a calm, quiet atmosphere during lessons, there is still a great deal of noise at other times. The

115

playground can be a very noisy, unpredictable place to be. Children tend to run in all directions, shouting, screaming, yelling and laughing. Their play may be undirected and random. There appears to be no order and this can be frightening for a child with autism. A child with ASD will require support in environments like this in order to be able to cope with all this confusion. This may be in the form of an additional adult such as a learning support assistant (LSA) or a specialized one-to-one support worker. A child may need an LSA's support more when they are out of the classroom than they do within it. A small nursery may provide a safe, quieter environment that may be easier for your child to cope with, but the transition to primary school can expose your child to much greater sensory issues. Lunchtimes in schools tend to be noisy and often entail many children crowded into one space, all talking at the same time, with the added noise of plates and utensils clattering and lots of movement as children get up and down. If your child has an issue with eating, then adding huge sensory overload to the situation is not going to help at all. You will need to ensure that your child is able to eat somehow whatever this entails, as a child with low blood sugar who is hungry will not be able to perform at all well. Although the ideal situation is for your child to eat alongside their peers, in reality this may not be possible and the school may need to provide a quieter, safe environment, which your child can tolerate at lunchtimes.

There are many ways in which you can help your child to become less sensitive to noise. You can start by exposing them very slowly and gently to noisy situations by visiting a school lunch hall for increasing amounts of time. Your first visit may last only seconds: you just open the door and look in. For your second visit, you may stay in the room for a few seconds before leaving. For subsequent visits, you should increase the time you spend in the room on a daily basis. To begin with, you may just expect your child to eat one small item and you may also try to arrange for your child to sit next to a friend they know and like who can be relied upon to help.

If your child cannot tolerate loud music, you may start off by playing music in the background at such a low level that it is almost undetectable, only slowly increasing the volume daily until your child can tolerate background music. All these things are very individual to each child and what works for your child may not work for another. Try to talk to as many people as possible for ideas so that you can try different approaches and find what helps you and your child. As with all things, the autistic spectrum is a very broad definition. These problems can be small and overcome fairly easily and painlessly, or they may be overwhelming and take many years and much patience to improve upon.

Self-Stimulatory Behaviour (Usually Known as 'Stimming')

You may observe your child doing strange repetitive actions or movements for no apparent reason, which may mean your child may have a degree of sensory integration disorder.

Stimming can take various forms and seems to provide some sort of comfort or pleasure for the child. Stimming is one of the defining symptoms or characteristics of autism and is listed in the *Diagnostic and Statistical Manual IV* as one of the diagnostic features of autism. Therefore, all children with a diagnosis of autism will be seen to stim to some degree. Stimming may also be observed in normally developing children, but not to the same degree that it is present in a child with autism. Stims can be visual, auditory, tactile, vestibular or to do with taste and smell. They can also be defined as being *excitatory*, which means they stimulate the child, or *inhibitory*, which means they are calming for the child.

Visual Stimming

A visual stim can be when your child holds an object very close to their eyes and appears to be observing it very closely and minutely. They may hold an object or just use their own hand as the object to focus on. They may pass the object back and forwards across their field of vision over and over again, almost appearing to look past it or even to look at it so closely as to appear almost cross-eyed. Sometimes they may go up to a static object like a table and put their eyes very close to it and then move slowly in front of it so that it passes their eyes repetitively and offers a different perspective. This is quite different from looking closely at something in order to obtain information about it, and it appears to be done for a different reason. It can seem as though your child is looking through the object and not really at it. It may be quite difficult to get your child's attention when they are engaged in this behaviour.

117

A visual stim can also take the form of watching spinning objects. For example, your child might spin a plate and seem to stare at the movement rather than at the object itself. In fact, many children with ASD enjoy toys that spin and light up at the press of a button, and will play with these for hours. The movement of sand or water can also create a 'stim' for your child. They may pour water from one cup to another or turn on taps just to watch the flow of the water. You may need to use drinking cups with lids as your child may not be able to resist the temptation of pouring their drink on the floor or table just to watch liquid as it pours. You will often observe a child with autism in a sand-pit filtering or dribbling sand from their hands over and over while not appearing to play with the sand in any real manner, e.g. building sand-castles. They may also feel compelled to throw sand for the same effect. They just seem to want to watch the sand fall, and may do this for long periods of time if left to their own devices. If your child is left to play alone and does not have the play skills in order to be able to play appropriately, then you may often observe them engaged in visual stims, such as lining up objects, e.g. toy cars, in rows or lining up similar objects in colour order to form patterns.

A very common visual stim is hand-flapping when a child flaps their hands quickly with very loose wrists. Your child may do this when they are over-stimulated or very excited about something, such as when watching a fast-moving piece of action on a DVD or at the cinema. Your child may also just stand still and flap their hands up and down very quickly for no apparent reason. If this is a visual stim, they will watch their hands as they do it and be uninterested in anything else going on around them. This hand-flapping is a very obvious sign to other people that a child may be autistic and for this reason it is preferable to try to prevent your child doing this in public as it can arouse negative comments. Your child may also hand-flap for other reasons and may be watching something other than their own hands.

Auditory Stimming
An auditory stim may take the form of a child repeating words or a phrase over and over to themselves, such as a familiar phrase from a favourite part of a television programme or film. This may be something reassuring for them to hear when they are feeling

stressed. They may not actually understand the words they are repeating, but perhaps feel comforted by the sound the words make. This is also sometimes known as 'scripting', when chunks of language are repeated verbatim with no connection to what else is going on around. Or a child may have been amused by the words and repeat them over and over to make themselves feel happy in some way. If your child is non-verbal, they may still repeat words over and over or make other vocal sounds. Some children may make high-pitched screams or other noises they like the sound of.

If a child feels anxious in a situation, perhaps due to what they can hear around them, then they may make a loud humming noise, which calms them and drowns out the outside noise.

One of my boys seemed to hum for pleasure and was unaware of himself doing it. He would hum as he pushed trains back and forwards repetitively only a few inches up and down a track, therefore indulging in at least two 'stims' at the same time: a visual one of watching the trains, and an auditory one of humming to block out all external stimuli.

Tactile and Other Forms of Stimming

Tactile stims take the form of habits that many people do to some extent, such as twisting strands of hair or biting their nails. Of course, people not on the autistic spectrum may also do these things in an absent-minded way or as a nervous habit. A child with ASD may do something tactile very often and for long periods. They may cause injury to themselves by continually biting their nails or the skin around their nails until the skin is broken.

One of my boys bites the base of the nail bed of his thumb and leaves it damaged. I have to keep a plaster on it to stop him from chewing and causing further injury.

Toe-walking can also be a form of tactile stim. In this, a child walks around on tiptoe and does not place their heels down on the ground when walking. A less known or proven theory is that toe-walking may be due to a bowel or gut problem such as constipation (*see* page 79), which may cause the child to walk in a certain way to relieve discomfort.

A child may also physically spin themselves around and around to create a sense of stimulation. This is known as *vestibular stimming* and is linked with the sense of balance. Other forms of vestibular stimming can be running around in circles, which has a similar effect to spinning. Pacing up and down a room can also calm or excite a child. They may do this repeatedly or for long periods of time.

The classic symptom of rocking is a vestibular stim. Your child may comfort themselves by rocking back and forth or side-to-side. This is one of the most well-known symptoms of autism and people with little or no knowledge or awareness of the condition will assume that your child behaves in this way.

Finally, taste and smell can also be stims. Some children sniff everything and may go up to people to sniff them. It may be that they have a very sophisticated sense of smell.

One of my boys could tell when someone familiar had used a new soap or deodorant or shampoo. Unfortunately for my boys, sniffing other people randomly is not an acceptable thing to do in a social situation, so I would have to mollify complete strangers on occasions.

Your child may also feel compelled to lick objects or to put them in their mouth – acceptable in a baby, but not in a grown child or young adult.

So, stims can serve different purposes for the person who performs them. One theory is that stimming creates a pleasurable state and so sometimes allowing a child to stim may be used as a reward. In this way, a child may be taught when a stim is acceptable, e.g. a toy that lights up and spins around may be given to a child for short periods of time after completing a task. You may choose to allow your child to stim whilst at home unobserved by judgemental strangers.

Stimming behaviours can greatly interfere with a child's ability to learn and with their attention. While engaged in a stim, they are unable to attend to another task or situation. They are also very much self-absorbed in their own world and feelings and disconnected to what is going on around them. It can be very hard to redirect a child who is stimming towards another task or action.

There are numerous ways to reduce or redirect stimming behaviours. A good behavioural programme will be able to help with this. An OT is the most appropriate and knowledgeable professional to advise on some of these techniques and to provide alternatives. This may be known as a *sensory diet*.

5

HOW TO GET HELP AND SUPPORT

The Need for Support

IF YOU ARE FORTUNATE, your immediate family, such as your parents and siblings, will rally round to be with you and try to understand what you are going through, and what this diagnosis means for you and for your child's future. To begin with, you will probably need this support. In fact, it is almost more important in the first few weeks to establish a source of emotional support than to sort out the practicalities of how you are going to look after your child. After all, before diagnosis you will probably have been caring for your child without outside assistance and, although it may have become increasingly a strain to look after your child, nothing in effect will have changed overnight. It is true that your emotions on hearing your child's diagnosis will probably go through an enormous change, but your child's behaviour will be much as it was before you knew the diagnosis. Therefore, you may need a lot of emotional support to get you through the first few weeks or months. Hopefully, your partner will be involved in all your future decisions in caring for your child and the two of you will support each other.

But not all relatives are supportive. You may find that you need a lot of patience when trying to explain how your child behaves and why. If you are going through a grieving process yourself, you may find it hard to be patient with relatives who do not (or cannot) understand what you are trying to tell them. Some may think it is all just a phase your child will grow out of with 'better parenting' and that you are making excuses for your child or your own parenting style. Some people are so wrapped up in their own lives that they are unable to spare time for those who need it, even if they are members of their own family. At a time when you feel you have 'lost' your child, you may also 'lose' the closeness with your own family. Autism seems to cause a ripple effect in this way and this can have far-reaching consequences.

So, what do you do if you have family who are not supportive or who are living in another part of the country far from you? What do you do if you are a single Mum or Dad without a significant relative or friend on hand? You will quickly need to find someone who can really help you through the initial emotions after your child has been diagnosed.

Friendship
If your family is unable to provide the love and support you need at this time, you will need the support of your close friends. It is a cliché, but one that is true: at times like these, you really find out who your true friends are. You may be surprised by who steps into the role of 'true friend' and who you lose along the way. Having a child with a disability really does change the dynamics of friendship and family. Over time you will meet other parents with children on the spectrum and will realize that they may offer you the best support in terms of empathy and true friendship. Parents of disabled children are touched in a different way in life; you will find that you will be able to laugh with them at things your child has done or at yourself and how your life has changed. Sometimes, other people are just not able to understand how you feel, but the parents of children with special needs will.

Because of what you will experience, you will change in many ways. Some things in your life will become more important and others less so. For example, you will not be so concerned over what career your child may have in the future, but will have a more simple desire for your child to have a meaningful life. When people say 'I just want my child to be happy', they may still be pushing their child towards a certain course in life, but if you say it, you will be coming from a place of pure emotion where you really, truly mean that you just want your child to be happy. Disability does make you stand back and assess life in a different way. Material things are no longer as important, but happiness is to be grasped at all times. While other parents are discussing their holidays or house prices, you may be concerned with fighting for funding for your child's education. There are many online groups to join up with if you have limited time to meet new people and talk. You can pop on and off your computer and post questions and get support from a wide range of people. There are groups for parents discussing certain types of therapies and general groups offering support and advice and, most importantly, friendship. Of course, online friendships are easier in some ways as you do not need to make actual appointments or leave the house. Also, the internet is so widely used that you will be able to converse with people with a broad range of experience, people who can offer you a great deal of expertise in certain areas. Nevertheless, ideally you will have the support of online friends *and* real, live people as much as possible for warmth, laughter and face-to-face interaction. That really is the best option.

Even if you are feeling desperate, try to remember that all the other mums and dads you contact also have a child with special needs, and respect their time. I have sometimes had to ask friends not to give out my contact number to other parents as I get approached so often that I could become a full-time counsellor if I spoke to everyone who wanted my advice. It's not that I don't want to help out another parent, but coping with four children of my own, all with ASD, is pretty much a full-time job most days. So, I am happier to answer emails and discuss things online as then I can juggle my own time. Also, when I have finally sat down at the end of a long day, sometimes I just don't have the energy left to talk to another parent.

Other Sources of Support

From Charities and Specialist Groups

In the UK, the National Autistic Society (NAS) is the leading charity for autism and Asperger's syndrome. The NAS offers information and support to families and carers of children with autism, adults with autism and professionals working in the field of autism. The NAS has local support groups, which run regular meetings for parents in the same area. There is usually a contact number of someone within your area who may be able to advise you personally on support available near you and what facilities your local borough can offer. They may be able to put you in touch with knowledgeable local members if you have specific questions such as those about schools in your area. You may also want to talk or meet up with other local families who may have a child with similar difficulties to your own. The NAS also runs a national helpline telephone service and its website offers information on almost every topic you can think of. Additionally, the NAS offers an extensive range of printed information leaflets, which you can download or request to be sent to you by post. The website also has a list of recommended books on topics linked to autism.

In the UK there are also many other children's charities and groups for disabled children, whether government-supported or independently funded. These may have regular drop-in sessions for parents of children with disabilities, offering therapies such as music or art in group sessions.

One of our local charities offers therapies like reflexology for the Mums while their children are taken care of in a play session. It is wonderful to have therapy for yourself while not having to worry about who is caring for your child. So you and your child benefit at the same time.

You may be offered short courses to teach you techniques to help your child, such as signing, Makaton or dealing with behaviours. Usually these courses will be subsidized or even run free by charities. Most charities and special needs groups run activities and therapies for your child to attend and separate courses for parents and carers to increase knowledge and help you to care for your child. Local authorities may also run short courses for parents to attend and you may be referred by your health visitor to courses such as the EarlyBird scheme, which is a course for parents of pre-school children who have a diagnosis of ASD and covers a wide range of topics. Try to attend some courses if you can make the time, partly because there is always something new to learn and partly because you will meet other parents in similar circumstances.

Special Needs Groups

Special needs groups often support parents of children with any type of disability, and you could find them equally supportive as they offer a wider range of experiences and not just experiences of autism. You may find you feel more comfortable with parents and children with a variety of difficulties. On the other hand, you may prefer to stick to groups who have children on the autistic spectrum. It is often easier to make new friends with the mothers of other disabled children than with parents of neurotypical children as you do not have to explain yourself and somehow you are all on the same wavelength. Hopefully, you may also find some like-minded playmates for your children at the same time.

> Some of my very close friends now are other mothers of disabled children. We don't sit and talk about our children all the time – we may not even mention them at all – but if we drop into the conversation that we have an annual review tomorrow, the friend knows instantly how important this meeting is without a lengthy explanation. We also seem to share a similar dark sense of humour, which is what gets most parents of children with ASD through some long, hard days.

The support of other special needs parents will become increasingly more important. You may not socialize as families as your children may not be compatible, but you will need other people in similar situations for advice and support. You may end up becoming good friends with people that you otherwise would not have met. Most parents make new friends when their children start at nursery or reception class, but your circumstances will probably be different. Opportunities for meeting new people may be very much less in your case. If your child does go to a mainstream school, you may be the only parent in your class with a child with autism and that can be socially isolating.

> Sometimes I think it is the parent who feels more like the alien in the playground or at the school gates than their child does. You will have to learn to develop a thick skin if you want to join in with a lot of the general parent discussions.

People might say to you that 'you are only sent what you can cope with'. This is just one example of the things people can say that can seem very patronising. It is almost as if it is alright for you to have a child with a disability as opposed to them having a child with a disability. It is not necessarily that they really believe these things themselves, but often they do not know what to say so they say the first comforting thing they can think of. People also have a need for everything to be alright in their world and if they can convince themselves that actually your life is not too bad really, then they do not have to worry about you.

When I told some people that my third son had also been diagnosed with autism, most said either 'Well, you must have expected that anyway' or 'Well, that's alright as you know what to do'. It was almost as though it was lucky that it was me having another autistic child, and not someone else! And I just wanted to shout, 'It's not my turn!' But if it's 'not my turn', then whose turn is it?

People can find it very hard to have true empathy for you as they may have no experience of what you are going through. Try not to let people hurt you in this way. There also will be wonderful friends out there who will be able to say the right things to you and you will soon learn who they are.

Coping with Social Situations Such as Parties

Ultimately, your friends may be those you turn to instead of family. You will need to be involved in social situations such as children's parties and will need acceptance from friends and other parents in order to be able to attend them successfully. It can be very hard when your child is not behaving like all the other children. Small children are very adaptable and do not have inbuilt prejudices, so other children will usually accept your child without judgement. If their parents accept your child, too, then life will be a little easier. Social isolation with a disabled child can be heartbreaking. If your child behaves badly at a party, you will need the back-up of friends there to defend you, if needs be. You may be too busy dealing with your child to be able to explain to a stranger why your child has behaved in a certain way. There is nothing worse than being 'told off' by another parent.

One of my boys was once a bit over-boisterous on a bouncy castle so another mother told me off very loudly in front of all the other parents for his behaviour. It was embarrassing and humiliating. I explained that my son had autism and she declared, quite dismissively, that he was a danger to other children and that he shouldn't be there at all. There was no reasoning with her. She ended up by shouting at me while I was trying to bring away all my children. When a second mother tried to step in and speak on my behalf, the first woman did not want to listen. I was very upset by the incident. My child had not injured anyone, but was made to feel unwelcome. However, some good did come out of this incident: that other mother who stepped in to defend me has now become a lifelong friend.

Not only is it hard to look after your child in a party situation, it can also be emotionally draining to watch other people's children having fun and enjoying the party while your child may be bewildered and not enjoy the experience at all.

So, social situations are a double-edged sword. You need to try to keep doing things socially as a family and your child needs to continue to be exposed to different activities and situations, but it can be so hard. Just watching neurotypical children reminds you of how your child should be and how your child is not able to be. You will sometimes feel as if *you* are the odd one out, not your child. Your child may actually be oblivious to other children and have no awareness of themselves and how they are, but this is heart-breaking for you. Your child may not have any desire or need to join in with other children while you will dearly wish that they did. To watch your child isolated from a group is very difficult. Your job now is to help your child to integrate in whatever way they can into any social situation, and this will not be an easy task. For your child's sake, you will need to be strong at times and to put on a brave face and try to make the situation enjoyable for your child.

I have come home many times and cried after an event. I hope my boys have not picked up on my sadness and that my false smiles have tricked them, too, but sometimes I fear not. Our children can be very intuitive.

If your child finds it very difficult and distressing to cope socially out of your home, you may soon find that special needs' settings are easier to tackle, at least initially. You may also need to find other methods of managing socially, such as planning ahead. So, rather than having your child attend the whole of a birthday party, including a performance by a magician or Punch and Judy man, you could arrange for your child to turn up for the earlier 'tea' part only. This way your child can take part in the party with their friends, but not have to sit through the later performance, which could be stressful for them. Playgroups are also good because you only need to stay for as long as you want and can manage.

> My boys always left nursery before the end of the session as they could not tolerate carpet time and the subsequent chaos of everyone leaving at the same time.

If you are able to leave your child at a nursery or party, you will need to ensure that you are there early to pick them up so that there is no anxiety about you not coming when they see the other Mums and Dads arriving. In reality, though, most children with autism will not be able to stay at a nursery or party without you or one-to-one support or, at least, without someone they know very well.

> For years, I was the only Mum who stayed with my boys at parties. I used to feel a bit resentful that all the other Mums were getting a break to go shopping or have a coffee and that I usually ended up helping at the party while I was the one who really could have done with a break.

If you find a special needs playgroup to attend, the volunteers or workers there will appreciate this when others do not, and hopefully they will try their best to give you a break. You may get the chance to chat to some other Mums and Dads in a similar position, or just be able to sit down for a welcome bit of respite.

Getting Practical and Financial Help

Financially, there is some help out there. Disability Living Allowance (DLA) and direct payments can help. However, sometimes it can take quite a bit of effort to find out where and how to actually get this help. You will find you need extra cash for all sorts of things.

Help with Childcare

Some practical help in the form of childcare and babysitting will be vital if you do not have family support. If you have other children, you may need two babysitters in order to go out and safely leave your children. Your child with autism may require one-to-one support just to be in the house, let alone to leave the house and attend an activity. This cannot be you 24 hours a day; you will burn yourself out. You may need help going out and about, particularly if you have other children with you, as you have only one pair of hands.

Twins running off in opposite directions can be hard enough to keep safe; twins with autism adds a whole new dimension.

If you have other children, they too need your undivided attention sometimes, so you may need childcare for your child with autism to enable you to spend quality time with their siblings. There are many times you need to be watching a school play, attending parents' evenings, taking your other children to activities when it may just be impractical to take your child with autism along, too.

If I dress my son in his coat and shoes to go out, do a round trip in the car to drop another child off, and then return home not having been anywhere, my son cries as he doesn't understand why he didn't get to go on an outing. Without enough language, how do you tell a child that the car trip has no purpose for them? Yes, a toddler will happily accompany you as just being with you and looking out of the window may be enough stimulation for them, but an older child will start to anticipate and associate going out with actually having a purpose for them, too. Therefore, I pay for childcare for my youngest to stay at home so as not to disappoint him when acting as a taxi for my other children.

Financing Therapies

You will certainly need funds for therapies, many of which may not be provided by the government. Or, if they are provided, they may be insufficient and you may have to join a long waiting list. You will want to get help as early as you can. Almost as soon as you have a diagnosis, you need to be getting as much therapy for your child as you can manage. The list of therapies on offer is almost endless, ranging from mainstream therapies like speech and language therapy, occupational therapy and behavioural therapies, to less well-known alternative therapies like sound therapy and approaches like the Hannen programme. Many people even go abroad for some therapies not yet available here. Although education should be provided as your child's right, in actuality it can take years to get the right educational support and, in the meantime, you may end up paying for it yourself. Even if you end up at a special needs' educational tribunal and win, there will be no compensation for all the educational therapy you yourself paid for and provided until the tribunal, nor for the legal expertise you needed in order to be able to win. Tribunals can be hugely expensive in their own right as you need to pay for expert opinions and reports and for those experts to speak on your behalf.

If you have not yet got a proper diagnosis and are on a waiting list, you can seek a private opinion (*see* page 28). This will speed up the process of getting help and support for your child but, of course, you will have to pay for any consultations, tests and reports. You may need to pay for a developmental paediatrician to diagnose your child and for an educational psychologist to assess and put some recommendations in place. If you do use practitioners in the private sector, always remain in the state sector, too, and do not refuse any appointments offered to you. There are situations where an opinion from a government-paid employee takes more credence than one from a private consultant.

Hidden Costs of Autism

Your child may be destructive and intentionally (or otherwise) destroy things. They may break toys, perhaps because they do not understand how to play appropriately with them. If a sibling's toys get broken, understandably that sibling will get very upset if the toy is not replaced. Your child may tear paper, scribble on walls, rip wallpaper, stain carpets and break things unintentionally. Although you will learn to remove precious items and try to keep fragile items out of reach, it is not always possible and things will get broken.

We once stayed in a friend's immaculate holiday flat and one of my boys managed to twist himself in the long curtains and pull the curtain railing off the wall, which meant an emergency call-out to a handyman to fix it before we left. The same son, aged two, also pulled a radiator off his bedroom wall, causing a flood in the room downstairs. The damage ended up being covered by insurance.

Children with autism are often fixated with water and will flood the bathroom if you turn your back for a minute. They may bail the water out onto the bathroom floor and damage the flooring. They may also leave taps running and walk away. If you have an outdoor tap, you might need to get a tap-head, which is removable, as otherwise they will be constantly playing with the water. Your garden will be flooded and any grass you once had will become a pile of mud. Your child may not understand the basic concept of right and wrong, and so telling them not to do something is ineffective.

Extra Cost of Practical Items
Items such as a larger buggy may be needed when your child grows out of the usual toddler-sized buggy. It may be necessary to be able to take your child out secured in a buggy if they have no sense of safety, which is very common in children with autism. There are larger disabled buggies on the market for older children but, of course, this is an additional expense. You may need a larger car seat or restraining seat belts to keep your child safely in their seat while travelling in a car. There is a specialist harness you can buy which even Houdini would find it hard to escape from – invaluable if your child is able to undo a seat belt and get out of their seat.

If your child is very sensitive to clothing seams or fabrics, there are specialist companies who manufacture seamless clothing. Most children with autism prefer to wear natural fabrics such as pure cotton, which do not itch or scratch (excepting wool, of course, which can be very irritating). You may need to seek out larger-sized clothing with elastic waistbands for children unable to manage zips and buttons.

Disability Living Allowance (DLA)
You will be entitled to DLA for your child once problems have been identified. You do not need to wait for an actual diagnosis to apply. The application forms can be overwhelming to complete so, if you

can, try to find someone to help and advise you when you fill them in for the first time. Completing one of these forms can also be time-consuming and rather depressing as you have to list every single problem your child has in every area of their lives and, when you see it all down on paper and have to think hard about every one of your child's issues, it can be overwhelming. A social worker or family support worker may be able to help you. Alternatively, there are benefits advisors attached to family support centres, or some charities who can go through the paperwork with you. It is essential that you take your time and fill in the forms with as much detail as you can to ensure that you get the maximum rate that your child is entitled to. Do not dismiss or underplay any problems that your child has: there may be things that you have learned to deal with and almost think of as 'normal', but all the time remember that when filling in the forms you are comparing your child to a neurotypical child of the same age. This realization, too, can be quite hard.

I don't have a neurotypical child and almost don't know sometimes what is normal for a child the same age and what is different and caused by my child's autism.

This is why you may need to take advice from someone who knows and understands the forms, and why you need additional help to care for your child over and above that required by other parents. The form often asks how many times a day your child needs help to complete an activity and how long your child takes to do this on average. Obviously, sometimes your child will cooperate and something like getting dressed may be done fairly effortlessly, whereas on other days it may take you hours to get your child dressed and out of the house. Therefore, you need to think carefully about what constitutes an average amount of time. It may help to keep a diary for a few weeks; you could even send it in with the forms. Write down the time it takes to do all the things asked on the forms. You probably multi-task, as we all do. You will find yourself trying to get your child to take their tablets while they are eating their tea and probably packing lunch-boxes and doing another child's homework simultaneously. The whole point may be that if you had additional help and, therefore, additional time for your children, you could concentrate on one child and one task at a time. The long-term effects of this would be that not only your stress levels would be reduced, but also that if you really focused on one task with one child, you may find they learn to do that task quicker.

Teaching one child to put on their shoes quietly and calmly can be a lot more successful than hunting for four pairs of children's shoes and trying to get all your children to put their shoes on all at the same time. But, owing to lack of help, hunting for all those shoes is something I find myself doing far too often!

There are also parts of the form that need to be completed by other people. If your child is at school, there is a section the school completes about the level of support your child needs. Your child's head teacher may also write to your child's GP or any specialist medical doctor your child sees. You also need to ask someone who knows your child well to fill in a short section. This person can be a carer or a friend or another health professional whom you have not already named elsewhere on the form.

Try not to be overwhelmed by the forms. You are entitled to financial help for your child, and this is one of the ways in which you should receive it.

When I had to complete two sets of forms at the same time for my twins, I allocated an hour at a time to fill them in. It meant that the forms took a few weeks to complete, but I was able to concentrate properly on each section at a time. Trying to complete them at one sitting would not be a good idea. As you can probably gather, I find the forms very hard work, but the resulting financial help is invaluable.

Once you send in the forms, if you are awarded DLA the payments will be backdated to when you applied for it. You are usually allowed a number of weeks to complete the forms – which you will need!

There are three rates payable – low, middle and high – depending on the level of disability of your child and the level of support they require. This is also based on whether or not your child requires help overnight. If your child wakes during the night or requires any assistance during normal sleeping hours, then this affects the rate of care to which you are entitled. The money is paid directly into a nominated account, which you choose on a monthly basis, and can be spent as you need. You do not have to account for what the money has been used for so you do not need to keep invoices, accounts and receipts. The money is intended mainly for childcare support for your child to be able to access activities outside the home and for help with personal care within the home.

Often the rate will be set for a few years, so once you start receiving the money, hopefully, you will not have to complete the forms again for a while. From time to time, your child may be re-assessed at random, and you may have to complete the forms all over again. If your child's condition improves or worsens, so that you think you are on the wrong rate, you can apply for a different rate again. These payments are not means-assessed and so everyone, regardless of income, can claim for them.

Mobility Allowance

There is also an additional mobility allowance available. This is for children who are more severely affected by their autism. Although it is seen traditionally as being for children who cannot physically walk or who have mobility problems, a child with autism may be eligible for this allowance if they are unable to go out of the house and walk independently. This can mean that an adult has to hold their hand and control them for their own and for other people's safety, or perhaps that they are too big or heavy to be carried but they cannot (or refuse) to walk unaided.

Again, try to get some advice when completing the forms for this allowance as autism is harder to explain than a physical disability. For example, if you were to write that your child is unsafe outside as they might run across a busy road, this could be interpreted as your child obviously seemingly able to walk unaided and so not having actual mobility problems. You need to be able to explain in a particular way that your child cannot actually walk unaided outside the home as they have to have a person holding onto them at all times. Often the problem may be that your child refuses to walk and due to their size you cannot carry them as you did when they were a toddler. You or another adult are, in effect, the aid that your child requires in order to be able to walk. You have to be able to prove some form of mental impairment as opposed to physical impairment. Your GP or another medical professional should be able to write a supporting letter on your behalf.

If you are not awarded the level of DLA to which you think your child is entitled, you can appeal against the decision. This may mean an assessment or even a tribunal of sorts, but it is certainly worth appealing if you think you have not been assessed fairly. Obviously, this would add yet more stress and administration so, ideally, get as much help with completing the forms in the first instance so you do not have to fight the decision.

Mobility allowance has two levels: lower and higher. In a younger child, it can be argued that they would be in a buggy or pushchair anyway and would need looking after by an adult, so you have to be able to prove that your child needs help over and above that required by another child of the same age. Mobility allowance is harder, therefore, to get for a child under the age of about three. A teenager who still requires the assistance of an adult to go out very obviously needs a much greater degree of help than other teenagers of their age. If you need an adult on a one-to-one basis for the safety of your child when outdoors at any age, then this too is very relevant, however young your child may be. In normal circumstances a parent or carer will often take more than one child out at a time. Indeed, anyone with two or more children of their own will expect to be able to take them out unaided and not need additional help for every outing. You may need an extra pair of hands just to go on the school run. All this needs to be thought through and written down.

Disabled Car Badge

If you do qualify for the higher rate of mobility, you can automatically apply for a disabled blue car-parking badge, also, without having to go through more assessments. Apart from being able to park in disabled spaces and other benefits, there are some financial advantages, too. You can apply for free annual car tax for your car if the car is used for the sole purpose of the disabled child and, if you live in London, for a one-off registration fee you can register and then do not need to pay the London Congestion Zone fees.

You cannot request a blue badge because of the cumulative effect of having more than one child with a disability, which does seem very unfair. I tried to apply for a joint badge for my children as trying to manage four children with autism really means we need a parking badge at times. The badges are only awarded individually to each child concerned and the badge is then in their name. So, each child has to fulfil the criteria on an individual basis.

Your child may therefore be eligible for both DLA and mobility allowance, all payable by the Department for Work and Pensions (DWP). You will get paperwork awarding the allowances. This can also be used as official documentation to prove your child's needs, for example, as proof of disability when visiting a theme park.

If you are in receipt of DLA for your child, you as a parent carer are also eligible for Carer's Allowance, which is a weekly payment paid monthly into a nominated account of your choosing. This allowance is to compensate for your not being able to work if you care for your child over 35 hours a week. Currently, you are entitled to earn a small amount a week after deductions while claiming this allowance, but do check this with your local Social Services Department. Again, Carer's Allowance is not means-tested.

For the Carer's Allowance, you only get a single weekly payment, which means that having more than one child with a disability does not mean that you are awarded twice the allowance!

You can also apply for your National Insurance payments to be paid as if you were self-employed. These payments count towards your final pension and are very necessary if you have given up work in order to care for your child.

Direct Payments

Through Social Services, you should be able to apply for direct payments. There is no fixed amount of hours for which you can apply. In reality, it depends on your Social Services Department and the finances it has available. The number of hours a week you may get varies greatly from one area to another. You can ask for hours for your child to be looked after, either at home or outside your home so that your child can attend an activity or go on an outing. Either Social Services can provide childcare for you or, in some areas, you can ask for the money to be paid to you so you can find and pay for your own carers directly. If you have the time and energy to recruit your own help, you may find it easier to receive the direct payments yourself and then pay different people to help you and your child. It may be that you need someone to accompany your child to a group like Cubs or Brownies, and this person may be a different person from the one who comes to look after your child at home while you go out to work. You do not have to spend the exact number of hours each week that you are allocated, which means you can accrue hours and spend them as you wish. You may want to save hours up and have a night away, or keep some for the school holidays when you need more help.

You may be able to get additional hours during school holidays and half-terms as a fairly standard allocation of three hours a week does not go far in the long summer holidays. Social Services may also be able to pay for your child to attend a holiday scheme. You will need to refer yourself to Social Services if no one else has done this for you already, and have a home visit and assessment from a social worker. It will be up to social services how many hours you are awarded. Some are much more generous than others. Even if you only get a few hours to start with, it is worth having as you may be able to increase the amount of hours you get at subsequent assessments. The money needs to be paid into a separate account and, unlike DLA, you need to keep complete records of how the money has been spent and for what purpose, and send in quarterly returns. You can receive help with this administrative process either from Social Services or through a charity. You are not allowed to use direct payments to pay a cleaner or someone to assist you personally, as the money must be used to pay for help directly for your child, e.g. a babysitter or one-to-one carer. In terms of applying for the payments, you do not have to fill in long forms like you do for the DLA. A social worker will come and assess your situation and may visit your child at home or observe them in another setting in order to assess how much help they think you may need. They will write a report, which you should be able to see and approve before it is finalized. The hours allocated will usually be reviewed at least once a year, but you can request another assessment if your circumstances change, or if there is a reason that you require more hours.

Discounted Entry or Tickets
Many theme parks, zoos and other places that you might like to visit often have concessionary rates for children with disabilities. It is

always worth checking before you visit. Often, carers go free so you will just have to pay entrance for your child. Sometimes you get an additional discount for your child. The letter awarding your child DLA can be used as proof that your child has a disability. You can also show your child's freedom pass if they have one. Some theme parks such as Legoland in Windsor will offer you an exit pass. This means that you do not have to queue for rides and can go straight to the ride exit. Children with autism find waiting and queuing very difficult and because theme parks recognize this, they offer a system where you can fast-track the queues. For this you may need to provide proof that your child's particular disability is autism, so check with the theme park before you go. You may be asked to bring along a doctor's letter or, if you have any other official document that states autism or ASD on it, this should be sufficient. These concessions are particularly helpful financially as otherwise you might have to pay for an additional adult's entrance fee if you require another adult to accompany you on outings to help with your child. It also means that you may be more willing to try out somewhere new if it does not cost so much in entrance fees. Other families may be able to spend hours at an attraction and get the full value of their visit whereas you may be able to stay only a short time because of your child's difficulties. An accompanying adult will certainly not have much time to enjoy the facilities themselves as they will be engaged in looking after your child, so it would be unfair if you had to pay a full admission price for them. Annual passes to local attractions and venues may also be worthwhile, both in terms of enjoyment and finance. Your child will have a chance to familiarize themselves gradually with a new environment and each time will enjoy the experience more. You can visit more often for short periods, which may suit your child better in the view of sensory issues such as noise and crowds.

Theatres and cinemas may also offer discounts. Some theatres offer concessionary rates for disabled children and for accompanying carers. You may be able to get half-price tickets for some shows. There is no official policy so, again, it is worth checking with each venue before you purchase tickets. For cinemas, you can register for a Cinema Exhibitors' Association card, which entitles you to one free ticket for a carer for each child in receipt of DLA to visit the cinema.

You can apply for a freedom pass for your child to use on public transport. This will entitle them to free fares. In London, these scan at the normal oyster card entrance-and-exit machines on trains and buses.

Other Sources of Funding

There are also some national charities to which you may be able to apply for help with funding some therapies or childcare or even equipment such as a computer, which your child might benefit from. Some charities have a threshold of income upon which they base their funding. Other local charities may be able to provide you with respite care, which you do not have to pay for. This is usually in the form of a carer who comes to your home to be with your child or to take your child out to give you a break. This may not be means-tested, but based on the need of the family. You may also be offered a place in a free children's club or activity for your child to attend. There will be other local charities in your area that might be able to help you financially with grants or with free services. Your social worker should be able to advise you on these.

For yourself, you may be able to apply for one-off carer's grants. These can be used for funding something that will benefit you personally, such as a break away from your child, some complementary therapies to help you deal with stress, or maybe driving lessons if you need to learn to drive!

Aiming High for Disabled Children is a government initiative. In some areas you can apply for an Aiming High short-breaks' grant for your child. This can be used to pay for entrance charges to theme parks, outings or towards a short-break or a holiday for your child. In other areas, the money is used to fund holiday schemes or holiday accommodation. The money seems to be allocated in different ways each year, so it is worth checking what is available in your area.

Looking after a child with disabilities is tough enough without the added stress of having to do this on a budget. There is help out there, so do ask. Every little helps.

6

THERAPIES AND EDUCATION

Which Therapy?

So WHERE DO YOU begin? How do you choose a therapy? Does it choose you, perhaps? By which I mean you may be offered a therapy of some kind by your local authority (LA) or other agency, and you will probably accept this therapy as, hopefully, it will be offered free of charge. You will also hear of a huge variety of possible therapies from numerous sources, such as other families or via the internet.

There will be so many options and different paths that you may choose to go down with your child. No pathway is set in stone and if something does not work for you, you can always stop and try something new. Some therapies, of course, need time to show any results, so the hard part may be trying to work out how long to stick with a therapy before changing or adding another. Each therapist will believe that the therapy they are offering is the best one possible for your child. Other parents may rave about a particular therapy and how much it helped their child; even so, it may not be the right one for *you* and *your* child.

One of the difficulties in choosing between potential thera-pies is that there does appear to be a huge industry now offering a wide variety of therapies and treatments. Some are clearly more mainstream and are widely accepted. Speech therapy, for example, has a proven track record of being beneficial to all children with a diagnosis of ASD. Speech therapy is not only offered to children with severe language delay, but also to children with Asperger's syndrome who may have normal language acquisition, but who can still benefit from speech therapy to help them learn important social cues and behaviour around speech and conversation.

There are many, many other newer therapies as yet perhaps scientifically unproven, but research may be in progress. Your choice will depend on how you feel about the more alternative therapies on offer and whether you believe they will benefit your child. Some parents become so desperate that they will try anything if a cure is promised. Others will surprise themselves by choosing a therapy that they would never have thought they would use, such as acupuncture (the stimulation of specific points on the body with fine needles). Sadly, there are people who prey on desperate parents and who may peddle so-called 'miracle cures' that may be expensive. To avoid this, you must be very careful when choosing any therapy, so ask advice from others and thoroughly check any claims first.

If we waited for all the potential therapies to be tried and tested and have a proven track record, our children would be grown up before many of these therapies got off the ground and were officially recognized. The research has to start somewhere and while you may not wish your child to be used as a guinea pig, if your child drastically improved as a result of a particular treatment you would be so glad that you did not wait for that therapy to be proven. Of course, you need to consider first whether the treatment could do any harm to your child, but very often it is more the case that your money has been wasted on a therapy that does not produce obvious results rather than it has done your child any lasting damage. A certain treatment may only produce a small gain where a different therapy may have more obvious results, but often you need to do many therapies in tandem that all work together.

So where do you start?

If money were no object and the LA or health authorities were willing to pay for any therapy that your child needed or could potentially benefit from, then that would make some of the decision-making much easier. Like most people, you will probably have a limited budget that you can afford to spend on helping your child. It is hard to know that there may be something that could really increase your child's potential or quality of life, but you cannot afford it.

In this case, first make sure that you take advantage of every possible therapy being offered for your child by your LA. You do not have to take up every therapy being offered. Indeed, you may well find yourself fighting your LA *not* to take up an educational provision offered to your child but want the LA to fund an alternative provision you prefer. Before you pay for any therapy yourself, you need to know what you are entitled to and what you might be entitled to with a bit of persuasion or a full-blown fight at tribunal. Unfortunately, there is no national policy on exactly what you might be able to get funding for. Each authority has its own special needs' educational budget and it has the power to spend that budget in the way it chooses. Some areas will have their own schools, which they maintain, and others will fund independent specialist schools, which may fall outside the area. You may be lucky enough to live in a more generous area, or you may live in an area with a smaller budget and known for trying to keep its costs low. As in health matters, special needs can be a postcode lottery. Some families have been known to move into a more sympathetic area, but once your child has been diagnosed you will want to get some support as soon as possible and applying for an EHCP or other educational help can be a lengthy process. If you decide to move, your child may end up waiting even longer just to begin the process while you buy and sell houses and perhaps have to re-arrange schools for your other children. Once you actually have an agreement for your child's education, it should be transferrable to another area. The reality is that this may not always be the case and the new area may try to amend or change the agreement.

Autism can seem like a parallel world in some ways in which your child's experiences and education may mirror the world of the neurotypical child, but not always be a complete part of it. Their path may intersect at some points with neurotypical children and at other times go along a totally different route. Our children will all grow up to become adults and at the back of your mind when choosing a therapy or making a choice about your child's education you should sometimes remind yourself about what knowledge or experience your child will need in order to be able to live alongside other adults in a normally functioning society. If your child is being taught maths, for example, you need to stop and think sometimes about how what they are being taught can translate to the real world. Our children with ASD need to be able to use money to buy items in shops, maybe manage a bank account and their own weekly budget. They may not necessarily need to know equations. A GCSE in maths might not be the best use of their time spent in a maths class, although it is gratifying to think that your child is able enough to take an exam at this level. Even though your child may still be very young, you should strive for them to reach their absolute potential while still retaining the thought of how their abilities will aid them in their future lives. Like all parents, your most important aim is for your child's happiness, both now and in the future. You do not know what your child's potential may be, so your aim is to do as much as you can to ensure that your child has the best future possible.

Without therapies – many of which we paid for by ourselves – I do not know or really wish to think about how my boys might have developed. I know that certainly they would not be anywhere near as able to function independently as they are now without having had the benefit of all those years of support and therapy. This makes me feel very bad for those parents unable to fund therapies themselves for whatever reason.

Therapies that Should be Offered by Your Local Authority or the NHS

There are therapies to which you and your child are entitled. These include speech therapy, OT, additional hours of one-to-one support in an educational setting or a place in a specialist school. In some cases, such as if you are running a home-based Applied Behavioural Analysis (ABA) programme or another home-based therapy, your home may count as an educational setting. If your child attends a special needs school or nursery, other therapies such as music, art or drama may be offered within the setting. If your child attends a mainstream school, some therapies, such as music therapy, will probably have to be self-funded. You may also be offered small group therapy courses for speech and OT in your area, but you should be able to get individual one-to-one sessions additionally if your child requires them.

EarlyBird Course

Most local authorities offer a course for newly diagnosed children and their families known as the EarlyBird course. This short course offers parents some support in recognizing and dealing with their child's behaviour as well as some strategies for helping them to start the process of learning about autism and what it means for their child and family. It is usually offered to pre-school children soon after diagnosis and runs for a few months and should be offered free of charge. It is not an ongoing therapy, but more something to get you started and focused if you are unsure of what to do next and need some support in the early stages. For some parents, it can be empowering and they are grateful to have something offered without a great deal of organizing involved. In other words, you do not have to do anything except turn up. For other parents, the course may be too basic because they have already started investigating different therapies and know what path they currently want to take.

If your child is very young, you may be offered help from the Portage team. Portage is a home-based educational service for pre-school children with learning difficulties or additional needs. You will receive weekly or fortnightly visits from a trained Portage worker. The main emphasis on this service is that the parents are the main carers and should be very much involved in their child's care. Portage can comprise of many different areas of help, such as mobility, feeding and play.

Speech and Language Therapy

If your child is pre-verbal or non-verbal at the time of diagnosis, you will need to find a way to communicate effectively with your child. You will certainly be offered speech therapy by your local health authority. This is usually allocated in a package of visits, perhaps an hour a week for a set period of time. The idea is that the speech and language therapist (SLT) shows you how to do the speech therapy with your child. They may work intensively with your child during the specified hour, but one hour a week is nowhere near enough therapy required for a child with communication difficulties. If you have relatives, or even friends, who can offer the time and the commitment, then you could ask the speech therapist if these helpers could sit in on a session so that they can also learn how to help increase communication with your child. Initially, your child may need to be taught eye contact before speech. This may involve playing games where your child is encouraged and rewarded for looking at someone before being given an item they desire. As strategies like this need to be reinforced all the time, it is vital that anyone looking after your child is aware of what you are trying to teach and that your child has 100 per cent consistency from everyone. In reality, that means that if you are trying to promote eye contact, your child has to be encouraged to look at the person they want something from at every opportunity. If your child were only encouraged to do this for the one hour a week with the SLT, the chances are that your child would take a very long time to grasp the concept, if at all. By involving everyone around your child in their therapy, your child will learn concepts much more quickly.

Even if your child has some speech, they will require speech therapy as all children on the autistic spectrum have social communication problems. It may be that your child appears to have normal speech, but has difficulties in reading body language and so misinterprets what someone is trying to say to them. They may also have problems in understanding facial expressions. How people use their bodies to express themselves in addition to speech is all part of normal communication. Some children may take speech too literally and interpret what has been said absolutely. They may not be able to grasp subtleties of speech and the ability to tell a 'white lie'. Children with autism can be brutally honest in the way that usually only very young children are, such as asking someone why they are fat or remarking on other physical attributes.

One of my boys once asked a girl I was interviewing when she was having her baby. She wasn't pregnant. It's a common error, but one that most people have learned not to ask if there is any doubt.

Children with autism may have problems understanding idioms such as 'It's raining cats and dogs' because they take everything literally. Even when you explain what these expressions mean, they may still ask why you said it if it was not true, or find it quite bizarre to use an expression that obviously is not correct.

It is very common that a child will talk on their own agenda, which means talking about what they want to talk about, often at great length. This may be on a totally unrelated topic to the question they have been asked, so having a joint conversation can be difficult. It only flows at all if the other person they are 'chatting' to is able to redirect the child, or correct them and perhaps change the subject. Without the ability to share and contribute to a normal conversation, a child with autism may be isolated and find it difficult to make friends. Another example of speech therapy in this situation could be the use of turn-taking games. A conversation should involve two or more people, each taking it in turns to speak, so playing turn-taking games is a skill that is a precursor to speech and having a conversation.

Sunday evening dinner can be quite bizarre in our house with four children all talking at once on their own agenda about whatever they want to talk about and not listening to anyone else. Apart from the noise levels, it is even harder when each of them thinks they are having a conversation with you and you are expected to answer and keep up with four different ongoing subjects! We try to introduce a topic to at least keep the children on the same subject, although often they are so eager to add to the conversation that they talk over each other.

Alternatives to Spoken Language

Sign Language

If your child does not understand language being spoken (known as receptive language) or have any verbal language themselves (known as expressive language), they may need the use of a different form of communication. This may be a form of sign language, often Makaton, which is designed to support speech. It is used alongside spoken language in spoken word order so that when you use a sign you also say the word as you would normally. A child who cannot communicate their needs will become enormously frustrated, resulting in many of the tantrums and behaviours exhibited by children with autism. Single signs can be taught one at a time, usually for things a child may commonly want, such as food items or a drink. As the child learns to speak, the signs will be dropped naturally. There is an official association for Makaton, which should be able to provide with you with further information. You should be able to attend an introductory course run for parents or professionals working with children with special needs. These courses are often run by independent charities. There should also be higher level courses once you know the basic signs. Some special needs schools also use Makaton, so one advantage can be that if you teach your child to use these signs at home, they will then be able to use them with other people who care for them. It is therefore better that you use a system that is widely known than make up your own signs, which will be specific only to you and your child.

Also, look out for children's television programmes that teach and use signing and are also watched by mainstream children. There is a group called Singing Hands who sing and sign children's songs. Makaton will not prevent your child learning to talk as spoken words are always used at the same time as the sign is made so there is a very clear association. If your child has very poor eye contact, some signs can be harder to teach as they require your child to look at you. If the sign can be made in front of your child's vision, such as using your hands to make a sign like the symbol for 'drive', then this makes it a bit easier. It can also be hard to teach signs if you have a child who is constantly moving and has poor attention skills. However, signing has been proven to be one of the most successful ways to encourage spoken language, so do not give up too easily or quickly if it seems an impossible task to teach your child to sign. As with many therapies, repetition and the amount of time and effort you or others put in does pay off!

Picture Exchange Communication System (PECS)

Although signs can replicate language to a high level, it is often easier to teach a child with autism to communicate their needs at a basic level using the Picture Exchange Communication System (usually known as PECS). This is another form of non-verbal communication that can be used to substitute speech. This is a very simple form of communication as it is very visual and easy to use. Most children with ASD tend to be visual learners and may not understand spoken language easily, but they will be able to recognize pictures.

The easiest way to start this system is to have photos of favourite items rather than symbolic pictures. For example, take a photo of your child's own cup with a drink in it. When your child wants a drink, they give you the photo of their cup containing the drink and you hand them their cup instantly, hence an exchange. You might start with just a few pictures until your child gets used to this system.

Because photos are an exact replica of what your child may

want, e.g. a specific type of biscuit or a favourite DVD to watch, the idea can be grasped much more simply as an exact exchange. There is no room for error or misinterpretation. You can put a small collection of photos into a box and let your child select the item they want you to give them. Of course, if you remove the photo of chocolate and that is what your child wants, then you might still set off a tantrum! So to begin with, perhaps just stick with photos of items you do want your child to ask for so that you will not have to disappoint them. Using PECS is very cheap to set up as you can download pictures or symbols off the internet or take your own photos of chosen items.

There are standardized cards that are used in PECS, but it may be easier to start off with your own laminated photos of objects, including drinks and favourite toys. The system can then be expanded to almost anything else that you or your child may need to communicate. For example, you might have a sign for singing, but then also have other pictures to represent different nursery rhymes or songs so that your child can give you a certain card in exchange for the song they want you to sing. The cards can be used to teach concepts and are often used in visual timetables. A visual timetable will be a large board divided into different parts of the day and visual symbols are placed in time order so that the child knows what is happening next or later on in the day. Picture cards can also be used in conjunction with each other, e.g. your child may request a sandwich using one card and then specify a filling such as cheese with a second card. They may also request to play a game with a certain person and so require the use of two cards or pictures to communicate this. An example of the everyday use of visual support in mainstream life is that sometimes children's menus will have photos of food for very young children to choose from and, of course, food packaging often entices us to look at it by using visuals to indicate what is inside.

In schools and nurseries, the cards used will probably be symbolic drawings or even simple black and white line drawings so that a picture of a cup can be used for a variety of drinks. Once your child has grasped the concept of a picture being a substitute for an actual item, they should be able to move on to more generalized pictures. The other advantage of a picture system is that if your child gives you a picture or photo of something they want, then you or someone else looking after them has no cause for error. If your child uses signs, you might be able to interpret what they are trying to tell you, but someone who does not know your child so well may not read the sign correctly.

You may find you use a combination of methods to aid communication and speech. It is hard to predict at a very young age which children will acquire a good level of speech in the future or which method will be the most successful for your child, so you may need to try various methods.

You will find these methods can help to reduce frustration enormously in a non-verbal child who is unable to ask for something they want or need.

Although my boys had hearing problems, when they were diagnosed the paediatrician explained that there is a very obvious difference between a child who is deaf and one who is autistic, even though both are unable to speak. A child who is deaf will try to tell you what they want by visual means, e.g. pointing, using gestures or perhaps even miming or acting out the action. In contrast, a child with autism will be unable to communicate verbally or non-verbally and very often does not point or have another way to indicate their needs. In this case, you need to teach them a method of non-verbal communication in the time before they (hopefully) start to talk.

Occupational Therapy

This form of therapy should be offered by your local health authority. Your child may be assessed by an OT when undertaking the process of diagnosis for ASD. However, if they have not been seen pre-diagnosis, they should still have an OT assessment and this may form part of the process you may go through at a later stage when choosing the education your child requires. Your child may be seen in a clinic or at school or nursery. In a very young child, the visits may be at home.

The definition of occupational therapy is to develop or maintain daily living skills for any child with a physical, mental or developmental condition. Under the umbrella term of ASD, a child may need help with any or all three of these categories. Autism is a developmental disorder that can cause serious anxiety and other aspects of a mental disorder. Children may also exhibit physical problems such as a delay in gross or fine motor skills. Autism is often viewed as just being a social communication disorder but, in fact, there are many, many other problems and issues which children with autism face, including medical, physical and psychological ones. This is the often misunderstood part of autism, which even health professionals may not fully acknowledge. Agencies offering services want to put autism firmly into the learning difficulties bracket so that the only service offered will be education. A child should be cared for within a multi-disciplinary team that looks after all aspects of the child's life, but in many parts of the country this approach is sadly lacking.

An OT should be able to adapt your child's environment if necessary or modify skills in order to maximize your child's independent functioning in everyday life. This may be by adapting a task to make it easier, such as using Velcro fastenings on a coat instead of buttons. It may also mean breaking down a skill into smaller steps that can be practised individually and increased over time, rather like starting with two- and three-piece jigsaws or puzzles that fit together, then progressing to puzzles with more pieces as each step is achieved. Sometimes, physical help may be needed in the form of perhaps a pencil with a grip attached or a rubber base to prevent a plate slipping. The aim is to increase independence with everyday living skills. A child with autism may have problems with fine motor skills and these problems may prevent them from holding a pencil or pen correctly and make writing difficult. They may also have problems cutting using scissors or doing up zips or buttons. Learning how to use cutlery is a basic skill that needs to be mastered in a society where most food is presented uncut in adult life. If your child eats with their hands they will not suffer malnourishment, but even to eat jelly or yoghurt they need to be able to manipulate a spoon to their mouths.

As older children, although my boys now eat a great variety of food, they still have problems with cutting up meat, and I often have to help them. Fortunately, they are still unaware that this could be viewed as them being 'different', but for a child who is more socially aware, this could cause anxiety or embarrassment in public. My boys also appear to have poor table manners because of the methods they sometimes use to eat their food.

Gross Motor Issues

Some children have gross motor issues: they may have been delayed in reaching developmental milestones such as sitting, crawling or walking. It is quite common in children with ASD that they have a degree of hypotonia (low muscle tone). This causes them to appear floppy at times. They may also be 'double jointed', which is an expression used to describe very loose or flexible joints known as joint hypermobility. So your child may have hypermobility caused by hypotonia. You may notice your child sitting in a 'W' position on the floor, basically sitting on their bottom with legs flat on the ground, knees in front and legs splayed to the sides. This should be corrected where possible. Children with hypotonia also find swimming harder as their back muscles may have poor tone, which leads to a weakness in core body strength. As a result, they cannot keep their backs straight and legs level with the water, and they may swim with their legs hanging down in an almost upright position. An OT should be able to offer a series of exercises to help strengthen certain muscles. The exercises may involve the use of large inflatable balls or other equipment. To strengthen back muscles, your child may perhaps be encouraged to play 'wheelbarrows', where you hold their legs and they walk along the floor on their hands.

The other area in which an OT will be of great importance to your child is in dealing with sensory issues. Children with ASD can be sensory seeking or sensory avoiding. Many of the behaviours your child has may be due to sensory processing problems or sensory issues (*see* Chapter 4). An OT may be able to devise a programme to reduce sensory stimulation, e.g. with brushing the skin lightly so that over time your child's skin becomes more accustomed to touch or pressure, and desensitizes. Some children need extrasensory stimulation to calm them down, perhaps in the form of deep pressure such as being wrapped tightly in a blanket or quilt and being hugged – quite a nice activity to do with your child! You may get advice on clothing such as sensory vests that weight your child down and help them to feel more grounded and safe. Some children like to be swung rhythmically, either in a swing or, again, wrapped in a blanket. A programme of regular sensory tasks may be advised, e.g. giving your child a rubber strap to pull hard against at regular intervals. This can help enormously with an older child at school who is having trouble sitting still and it can help them to cut down on fidgeting or moving around restlessly. Sometimes a child will be given a small object or toy to hold or squeeze during lessons so that they can pay attention to what is being taught without being overly distracted by the need to find something to fiddle with.

It may be that your child needs to do some exercise at regular intervals, perhaps in the form of jumping, running or stretching throughout the day. Boys in particular benefit from regular physical exercise even if they have no special needs at all. A child who is unable to sit still may be helped by the use of a sensory cushion to sit on that stimulates them and prevents them from having to move around in order to gain the sensory stimulation they need. An OT may visit your child at home to advise on certain exercises and things you can do when at home to aid your child. OTs are often involved in problems at school, such as with poor attention skills due to sensory issues. They will also be able to help with fine motor skills, which may be affecting a child's handwriting, or self-dressing skills, which can also be a problem as children need to dress and undress at regular intervals during the school day.

Other Therapies

There is a huge range of other therapies on offer, many of which you will have to pay for yourself or try to seek funding for.

The difficult part is choosing the right therapy for your child from such an extensive range. Even if you had sufficient money to be able to afford any therapy you wanted, you would still have to research and choose which ones to use. Some therapies can be carried out in conjunction with each other, e.g. an educational programme alongside biomedical intervention. You may be able to set a few therapies in place at the same time, but you need to be wary of overloading your child with demands and information. Life can be stressful for a child with autism and you may need to take it gently and introduce things at a slow pace. There is no miracle cure and certainly no quick fix. Many parents work tirelessly for years to enhance their children's quality of life and many are very successful, but it takes time and physical and mental effort to do so. Occasionally, you will hear of children who have 'recovered'. This is a term used for a child who is seemingly 'cured' of their autism. But be wary of anyone trying to sell you a system or therapy promising recovery. It is debatable whether recovery is truly possible. Could it be the case that the child who is now 'recovered' was misdiagnosed, or mislabelled at a young age? Could the child have learned to hide or mask any outward signs that may indicate they have a diagnosis of autism?

Different children do well with different therapies and sometimes it is simply a case of trying out something to learn whether or not it will be effective for your child.

Behavioural Therapies

Applied Behavioural Analysis (ABA)
ABA is the most well-known and researched behavioural therapy. This is the umbrella term and is used to cover programmes such as Lovaas, Verbal Behaviour (VB) and Natural Environment Training (NET), which are all different types of ABA.

ABA originated in the USA and has been used in the UK for the past twenty years or more. ABA is based on Skinner's findings that the consequence of behaviour affects the future happening of the behaviour. This is in contrast to Pavlov, who identified conditioned responses that become reflex actions. The earlier programmes were also called *behaviour modification*. The science of behaviour covers the basic principles of behaviours and the applied science is known as ABA when teaching is put into place to teach or modify behaviours.

The originator of ABA programmes in the 1960s was Ivar Lovaas. The very early programmes advocated the use of aversives (i.e. causing the avoidance of an item, situation or behaviour by using an unpleasant or punishing stimulus). This would mean that a child would be punished in some way for doing something the teacher wanted to stop them from doing. In recent years, this use of aversives has been amended and excluded, but ABA programmes are still looked upon by many as being detrimental to children because of this past history.

Although there is now documented research to prove that early intervention in the form of an ABA programme is the most effective therapy, there is still reluctance on behalf of many local authorities (LAs) to fund this therapy without a big battle, usually ending up in tribunal. It is expensive to run an ABA programme and some LAs do not want to pay for it. If a longer term view were applied – one that recognized that most children who have had ABA therapy have improved greatly – then perhaps funding would be more readily available. Unfortunately, the education budget does not consider the social services budget of a child in maturity who will require care as an adult. In fact, the long-term care costs of a child who has had the benefit of a well-run ABA programme may well be reduced as a result of that child's improvement, and this should more than cover the cost of the original therapy. However, this is not currently considered, so if you are thinking about ABA therapy for your child, you need to be well prepared with money, determination and energy. You may get no support or help from your LA to set up and run a programme. Indeed, be prepared for hindrance rather than assistance. There are a few ABA schools in existence, but you will probably need to fight for funding for a place at one of these as nearly all such schools are independently run, not by the authorities. Ideally, a programme should be set up and started at as early an age as possible, or soon after diagnosis. A programme of shorter hours can be commenced from the age of two upwards. The younger you start a programme, the more successful it is likely to be. Most programmes are started with pre-school children and it is known as an early intervention, but it usually continues throughout primary school and sometimes into secondary school, too. The majority of programmes, though, are with very young children and are mainly home-based.

An ABA programme is usually run by a consultant who should have the relevant degrees and qualifications in behavioural therapy (usually a psychology qualification plus a further qualification in ABA). There are many consultants to choose from and it is important that you pick someone you feel comfortable with, so talk with some other parents first to get references and recommendations. You can run a programme through a provider, who will send to you a consultant and perhaps a supervisor on a regular basis and help recruit and train tutors. Although this takes away some of the administrative work, you are paying for this service and an ABA programme is expensive to run without additional overheads. If you choose to run a programme independently, there are a great many consultants who work in similar ways but who may offer a slightly different service, such as more regular workshops or support beyond these workshops if you have problems at other times. A consultant will usually visit and run a workshop for a day every few months.

A programme supervisor may visit every two or three weeks depending on how often you need them, which may be dependent on how quickly your child progresses and how often the programme needs amending and moving on to the next stage. Owing to financial costs, some families choose to have just one level of supervision and may find a more experienced supervisor or junior consultant to manage their programme and have perhaps a monthly meeting. The day-to-day programme is carried out by trained tutors who work on a one-to-one basis with your child. This is the beauty of the programme and why it is so successful. The programme is tailored exactly to each individual child and moves at the pace of that child. This is also the reason why the programme is expensive to run as you have to pay for your child's one-to-one tutoring plus their supervision plus regular team meetings (which everyone working with the child will need to attend).

An ABA programme usually runs for approximately 30–35 hours a week. This seems to be a lot of hours, but you must consider that whereas a neurologically typical child will learn from their surroundings every hour they are awake, a your child with ASD may learn only when you are actively teaching them. Conversely, it has been proven that if you try to do too many hours (over forty hours a week), a child's learning ability will diminish, probably as a result of overload. There is a fine balance between giving your child the maximum hours to benefit them and overdoing it so that they cannot absorb what you are teaching. Due to lack of funding, sometimes parents do opt for fewer hours per week.

A good, well-run programme should be about your child enjoying the sessions and looking forward to their tutors arriving. All parents need to be committed to being actively involved in their child's programme. Sometimes parents themselves take on the role of tutor and run their own sessions, but many choose not to blur the boundaries between being a parent and being a tutor. If your child has severe behavioural issues, it can be hard to remain impartial and not get emotionally involved when your child has a meltdown. You have to live with your child for twenty-four hours a day; a tutor comes for a limited amount of time and can walk away at the end of a session. Of course, you need to know exactly what the tutors are doing within their sessions and what behaviours they are working on so that you can maintain the programme between sessions. Any approach taken needs to be 100 per cent consistent so that both you and your child's tutors react in the same way to any behaviour. You will also need to know what words your child is being taught so that you too can find ways to encourage those words, although you may not do it as intensively as a tutor would. For example, if your child is being taught two colours, red and blue, the tutor would introduce those colours in as many situations and uses as possible. They might play with red and blue Lego bricks, draw with a red or blue pencil, go outside and spot red and blue cars. You need to know that those are the two colours currently being taught so you too can add them in where possible.

An ABA programme consists of many different aspects. It teaches communication skills, whether verbal in the form of spoken speech or non-verbal in the form of signing or the use of PECS. You may also have an SLT within your team to offer regular input and advice. Speech may be taught in very specific ways. Language is broken down initially into very small parts so that the first words are usually single items that a child strongly desires, e.g. a biscuit. Once enough single words have been acquired, language can be expanded to two words such as 'want biscuit' and then finally the three words 'I want biscuit'. The words taught should be those that really motivate a child to want to speak, whether that means food or favourite toys or anything else.

Much of the emphasis of an ABA programme is on reinforcement, often in the form of rewards. A child will not be motivated to do something if there is not much in it for them. That can mean they get an actual reward, e.g. a star for their wall chart, or that they are rewarded by getting what they asked for, e.g. a drink. Your child may be happy to do a task for verbal praise alone or lots of positive reinforcement, which might mean clapping and cheering and telling them how well they have done. Tailor your child's reward to suit your child.

Of course, one of the main aspects of an ABA programme is addressing behaviours. In order for your child to function well in society, they need to be able to understand some of society's acceptable parameters. No one is expected to be perfect, but in order to fit in there are certain limits in behaviour. Some very obvious examples would be that in our society we wear appropriate clothing and do not walk around in public naked after a certain age. We might wear very little at the beach, but taking off your clothes in a public place that is not a gym or swimming pool is not acceptable. People expect to be able to go to the cinema or theatre and enjoy watching a film or play uninterrupted by others talking. We need to be able to cross a road safely and understand the rules of traffic. The list is endless and, although eccentricities are acceptable and not everyone wishes to conform to the norm, there are some situations in which your child will be expected to behave in a certain way. One of your tasks as a parent is to help your child achieve this.

You may not wish your child to be forced to fit into a certain mould, but if you wish your child to be happy, then there are some behaviours they may need your help with to address. After all, most behaviours happen because your child is unsure, anxious or unable to communicate properly. Therefore, working through the causes of behaviours and trying to solve them is a large part of any behavioural programme. There are many different methods that can be used and usually only one pattern of behaviour is worked on at a time. There may also be varied causes for the behaviour, e.g. if your child bites objects, this may be due to frustration or it could be due to something organic like toothache, where biting could be relieving the pain. So you might need to try to identify when your child bites and why. If your child wants something they cannot have and you have to say 'No' and then they bite, this is probably due to frustration and anger. But if the biting is a random action and seems to have no cause or reason for it, then it may be caused by a physical problem such as toothache.

Teaching a method of communication at the same time is, of course, hugely important as some of your child's behaviours will be due to an inability to communicate properly. If your child is hungry but cannot tell you or ask for food, they may have a tantrum. You will react by trying to guess what it is they want and will offer various things, perhaps a biscuit or a drink. The next time your child is hungry, they will have a tantrum again as this produced what they wanted last time. Thus, a pattern of learned behaviour is built up. If your child can be taught a word, symbol or sign for being hungry, they will learn that this is a much more effective and less exhausting way to get something to eat. This can have a huge impact on their lives and your own. A child having a tantrum in the middle of the street is awful for everyone involved. However, do not worry about the general public and what they think: for you and your child, a tantrum is equally upsetting.

An ABA programme should be able to work on all aspects of your child's life, including behaviours, communication, socialization and play skills. Everything taught will be broken down into small stages and adapted to your child's individual needs. Progress can be as fast as your child is able to learn and develop.

ABA tutors should have some previous experience of working with children. If they do not have knowledge of how neurotypical children develop, speak and play, how can they teach your child to do so? Although there are highly qualified courses available in ABA, in reality only the supervisors and senior tutors may have these qualifications. Some tutors may have psychology degrees or teaching qualifications, but the most important quality is a genuine love for children and the wish to really improve their lives. The tutor needs to be able to make learning fun for your child, so they need to have good play skills and a positive outlook on life. It can be great fun working with a child on an ABA programme but at times it can also be very challenging.

Initially, you will have to fully fund a programme yourself without any finance from your local authority (LA). This can make ABA a very expensive therapy to commit to. There are hardly any LAs willing to fund a programme without a battle, even though ABA is proven to be the most effective therapy for a child with autism. In addition to the expense, the LA has to trust the parents who are effectively running the programme to run and manage it successfully. In reality, this can mean that you may have to fund your programme for at least a year. You will then most likely face a tribunal to try to secure funding for the programme to continue. You will have to pay all your legal costs plus reports from expert witnesses, such as an educational psychologist. Even if you win against the LA and are granted funding, you will receive funding only from the date that you are awarded the funding. So you will not get any backdated funding or your court/tribunal costs. You need to ensure that you have sufficient funds of your own to keep the programme going until this point, at least.

We had already re-mortgaged our house for our twins' ABA programme and couldn't beg or borrow any more money, so for the first year of running our third child's ABA programme, we had two lodgers in our house to fund the tutors' pay and tribunal costs. This meant the twins having to share a bed in the smallest room and the presence of two extra adults in our house on top of three sets of tutors coming and going on a daily basis. It was like running a school and a B&B all in the one house. We had to do it, though, as we had seen how much progress our twins had made and knew we had to do the same for our third son. It was a very difficult year before we made it to tribunal and was made even harder, of course, by having to come to terms with the fact that our third, beautiful, smiling boy also had autism. But looking back, I would do exactly the same again, without a doubt.

An ABA programme is often run for between thirty and thirty-five hours a week. Usually, your child will have a morning and an afternoon session, Monday to Friday. You will probably start with a team of three or four tutors who work a few sessions each a week. Some families additionally have a session at a weekend, perhaps on a Saturday morning. The programme is home-based to begin with, until your child has bonded sufficiently with their tutors. The aim is for your child to be able to attend nursery or mainstream school accompanied by their one-to-one ABA tutors. This may be only on a part-time basis. Because a consistency of approach is required to be most effective, the people who accompany your child need to be trained in your child's individual programme. It would be too confusing and would prevent your child from achieving targets and goals if the people looking after them were unfamiliar with the programme. This can create problems as some nurseries and schools do not like staff who are not part of their school or nursery coming and working in their environment. A head teacher usually recruits all the staff and your tutors will not have been recruited by the school, but by you. This is fine while your child is working at home. However, when working in school or nursery, you and your child's tutors need to be sensitive to the needs of the school or nursery and work very much alongside them. Some places may refuse to accept your child with their current tutors, so you need to research carefully which schools will be more open to your child coming and going with their own staff.

Your child's tutors should have training in the methods used by your consultant or supervisor. However, having a degree in ABA does not automatically make you the best tutor.

> In the past, I have employed tutors from all walks of life. Alongside the teachers and psychology graduates who taught my boys, we have also employed a stand-up comic, a few dancers and various musicians.

You will need three or four tutors in your team. This helps your child to learn in a more flexible way. Each person works slightly differently and this will prevent your child becoming too rigid and only being able to do things in the way that a specific person does. It will also help when introducing others like teachers that your child is not too dependent on one person alone. There are not many courses so most families train their own tutors up and on the job using more experienced tutors to work alongside and train the new ones. For most parents, one of the hardest parts of running a programme is finding, recruiting and keeping good tutors. It is said that you lose approximately 50 per cent of the tutors you take on in the first few months. It will be up to you to place advertisements, interview, train and pay all your tutors. You may not have run a business before, but you will soon feel like you are running one and will probably have to set up the whole programme without help, and then move on to fight the LA for the funding to continue to keep it running. An ABA programme may be very beneficial for your child and in the very long term cause you fewer problems, so that in five or ten years' time your child is much more able than they might otherwise have been. But it really does take a lot of energy and is always very stressful for the parents to manage.

> I ran three full-time home-based ABA programmes for eight years and it has certainly taken its toll on me, mentally and physically. I also had the inevitable three tribunals in order to gain funding – this on top of running the programmes is more than one parent's work. You really end up by putting your own life on hold in order to do the best you can for your child or children, but you should also bear in mind your own mental health in doing so. I could write a whole separate book on the ins and outs of running an ABA programme. The programmes we have run have been the most effective things we have done for our boys, but they have also been the hardest, most stressful experiences I have ever had to go through. Despite the effect it has had on me, I am currently running

my fourth son's programme because I still believe it truly changes the outcome for my children – for their futures.

There are some dedicated ABA primary schools now and a few secondary units. These use ABA methods to teach children and all teaching is done on a one-to-one basis within a small classroom. The advantage of a school is that you do not have to manage a programme yourself, so your child will be educated every day whatever happens. On a home programme, if your tutor takes a day off sick or for holiday or leaves your programme before you have had time to replace them, then you have to look after your child all day. They will miss valuable therapy time unless you have no other children and no paperwork and no housework and you are a great therapist yourself! A school will be able to take your child every day. This is a big consideration if you are a working parent and need to rely on being able to get to work. You will also not have to worry about employing tutors and all the day-to-day management of your child's programme, so clearly this is an easier option.

However, depending on your child, there may be a negative side to an ABA school. One of the principles of an ABA programme is that it is intended for use alongside mainstream teaching. When your child is very young, one of the most important aspects of any programme is that your child is encouraged to integrate and mix with other children. Literacy and numeracy skills can be taught at a later stage than for other children, but the ability to socialize is fundamental to your child's happiness and well-being in the future. So, many parents prefer to keep their child in a mainstream setting for the first few years just for the socializing element. The hope is always that your child will be able to function in mainstream life as they grow older, whether or not they have academic abilities. For the future, this means that your child may be able to cope in the everyday world we all inhabit, and be able to go shopping, watch a film in a cinema or even enjoy a drink in a pub. Obviously, the younger your child is exposed to mainstream life, the easier it will be for them. If your child is able to mix with other children without becoming distressed and they are able to function in a mainstream setting, albeit with help, then you may want to consider an ABA home programme with mainstream inclusion. If, however, your child cannot cope in mainstream nursery or school for various reasons, then an ABA-based school may be a good alternative.

> My four boys have all had one-to-one tutors at home from the age of two or three and then were gradually integrated into mainstream nursery, followed by primary school accompanied by their tutors. Although it was hard for them because they found it overwhelming at times, it gave them the opportunity to mix in mainstream society with a suitable peer group and to learn at first hand appropriate social interaction. Young children are much less judgemental than adults and will accept your child for who they are and not for what they can or cannot do.

Your main consideration must, of course, be the overall well-being of your child. It would be unfair to expect any child to cope in mainstream if they cannot access any learning there as they are too overwhelmed by all the noise, activity, etc. An unhappy, stressed child will not benefit from being in an environment they cannot tolerate.

There are other individualized programmes that are not so well known but which may be more suited to your child. ABA may be the right approach for some children and their families, but for others, both the parents and the children, it might just be too stressful. If you are not happy with your programme, ask to visit some other programmes and talk to other families, different providers may work in a way more acceptable to you so consider this before giving up on a programme.

Another option to consider is a specialist ABA school. These are mainly based in London as they are still a relatively new concept in education. At one of these schools, each child will have a one-to-one trained ABA tutor within a very small class. The class then additionally has a supervisor/class teacher who oversees the one-to-one tutors so that there is a very high level of support for each child. Again, each child's programme will be individualized according to their needs. The advantage of an ABA school is that as a parent you do not have to run and manage your child's programme and you do not have to rely on a full team of tutors turning up to work with your child every week; a school will always be able to accommodate your child. For mothers who would like to try and work, this is really the only solution as mothers running a home ABA programme will inevitably find themselves without tutors for days or weeks at a time due to sickness, absence, lack of tutors, etc. It is hard to emphasize what a huge commitment running a home programme is. With a school, you will have the reassurance that your child will always be cared for and taught at the specified times. Some ABA schools may also cover secondary education, too.

If your child finds socializing with mainstream children too stressful, or is unable to be in a mainstream setting for any period of time due to one of any variety of reasons, then a specialist ABA school may be a kinder environment for your child. Your child will be helped to integrate and socialize at their own pace and will be placed in groups according to their level of interaction and communication. The level of support at an ABA school will also be very high, with a corresponding staff:pupil ratio.

One of the problems with choosing a specialist school of any kind is trying to secure funding for your child to attend. In reality, if your LA has any other provision to offer that it deems adequate, you may have a huge battle in the form of a tribunal on your hands in order to win the funding. ABA schools are nearly always independently run and some will not take children privately funded, which means that even if the parent is willing or able to pay, the school will only accept children funded by their local LA.

Mainstream or Not?

The final consideration is whether you wish your child to be educated alongside mainstream children or with other children on the autistic spectrum. This is often a very personal matter about which some parents feel very strongly one way or the other. In a democratic society, it would be nice to think that a parent could make that decision themselves, but the authorities may wish to intervene and make decisions based on research or, indeed, on cost. Many parents opt to try to educate their child in mainstream to begin with and, if this is not successful, they may then choose to withdraw their child from mainstream school and request a specialist provision. It is often easier for a child to start in mainstream from the beginning than to change back to mainstream from a special needs school at a later age. However, this is always very individual to each child. Some children are not ready for a mainstream environment at a very young age, but after some therapy and intervention they are more able to integrate slowly into a mainstream environment. You may need to take professional advice on what choices you make, but you should also be guided by your child and their well-being and happiness. Your dream may be for your child to be in a mainstream school, but if the reality means that they are unhappy and not flourishing, they will not be learning. So you may need to consider other types of educational provision. A child who is doing well with an ABA programme, but finds other mainstream children and all the commotion in a school too much, may benefit more from being in an ABA specialist provision.

SCERTS®
The acronym SCERTS is a registered trademark and stands for:

Social Communication – the development of spontaneous and functional communication
Emotional Regulation – to develop a well-regulated emotional state in which to enhance learning and to cope with everyday stress
Transactional Support – support to modify and adapt the environment and tools to support learning, e.g. PECS

SCERTS is a fairly new therapy devised in the last five years or so by a team that includes an SLT and other special needs therapists. It encompasses other known therapies, including ABA, TEACCH, Floortime and RDI. It promotes child-initiated communication and is best used in an environment in which children can learn from other children as role models. It may be adapted for use in the home in a similar way to an ABA programme or used in schools. Ideally, it is utilized in mainstream settings where children can learn from good speech and language role models. It differs from ABA in that it promotes child-initiated communication in everyday activities and the ability to learn spontaneously. It is therefore a more child-led programme than an ABA programme, which is often adult-led and -initiated. A child's progress is monitored systematically and regular targets are set and charted, again in a similar way to an ABA programme.
    You may find that your consultant or supervisor will adapt your

child's individual programme using a mix of the SCERTS approach and some aspects of a verbal behaviour (VB) – a version of ABA – programme and maybe some relationship development intervention (RDI) or intensive interaction (II). These are all valid approaches that can be used together, and a very experienced consultant should be able to draw on aspects of these similar approaches and adapt your child's individual programme to suit your child's needs. A rigid approach is not healthy when working with a child with autism as their needs vary so much. The most important aspect is that your child is able to learn in the way that best suits them and their learning skills, and not what the programme is called. Some people find they may need to vary their teaching styles enormously depending on the child they are teaching. Obviously, all teaching needs to be fun and enjoyable for the child so that the child wants to learn and is motivated to learn.

There are many other lesser known therapies, some of which are outlined here.

Relationship Development Intervention (RDI)

This is an intervention that is intended to improve social and emotional relationships. It is a trademarked treatment programme and there are specialists trained to teach the method to families as it is very much a family-based programme. It aims to increase the ability of a child to form relationships. This method is often used in conjunction with other methods.

Intensive Interaction (II)

Intensive interaction aims to develop the fundamentals that precede speech development. These include physical contact and enjoyment of being with another person, using and understanding non-verbal communication such as eye contact. It is a highly practical method and requires no specialist equipment except a sensitive person to interact with.

This method was developed based on the first year of a baby's life and how that baby learns the fundamentals of communication. It is often used with pre-verbal children, but can also be used with those who have developed speech. The sessions should be frequent, intense and fun.

The HANDLE® Programme

HANDLE® is another registered trademark, the acronym of which stands for Holistic Approach to Neuro-Development & Learning Efficiency. It was devised by a lady called Judith Bluestone, who herself was born with severe sensory issues.

The programme comprises a series of exercises to share with your child to enhance their learning. One of its basic precepts is that a stressed system is not a good state in which to learn, so all the exercises are intended to calm the sensory system.

Son-Rise

This programme was devised in the 1970s by the Kaufman family for their son with autism. It is a system for parents to use when interacting with their child and the emphasis is on creating a stimulating, loving and nurturing home environment. One of the more controversial aspects of it is that it encourages parents to join in with any ritualistic or repetitive behaviours (unlike other programmes, which work to eradicate these behaviours). The controversy is whether these behaviours should be worked alongside, tolerated or removed. For example, if your child makes a strange noise, you may wish to ignore it or take active steps to prevent your child from making this noise. In a Son-Rise programme you would join in with your child and perhaps make a similar noise in response. This may be the beginning steps of communicating with your child and entering into their world instead of trying to make them part of our world as we see it. Your child may be making that noise in order to communicate something to you. By joining, you will be bonding with your child. From there, you may be able to adapt the noise to something more appropriate, such as a single word that tries to convey what your child may be wanting to tell you.

Although in a Son-Rise programme there are concepts to be worked on, such as extending time spent on an activity or increasing eye contact, there are no demands as such placed upon your child. The therapy aims to increase your child's own awareness and confidence by a situation of total acceptance. This means that there are no good or bad behaviours, as such; whatever your child does is acceptable and the therapist will join in with them in a non-judgemental way. The basic idea is to join in with your child's world in order to encourage them to reciprocate and join in with your world.

TEACCH®

Some schools use Treatment and Education of Autistic and Related Communication Handicapped Children (commonly referred to as TEACCH), which is a structured teaching programme designed to help integrate those with autism into the wider community. It is not a single method or technique, but encompasses many aspects of helping a child with autism by doing things such as reducing key autistic behaviours and adapting the environment to suit a child's needs.

Biomedical Treatment

Some people now believe that autism may have a link to medical issues and as such requires expert medical treatment. This is known as *biomedical intervention*. You may want to consider the biomedical route and try to treat some of your child's physical or behavioural problems in this way. These can include specialist diets, nutritional supplements and other therapies. For example, biomedical treatment to help your child's digestive system may be beneficial to some children and may remove a source of pain or discomfort for your child. The removal of pain could result in fewer tantrums and an increased ability to interact and to learn, and not just the obvious results of perhaps a more normally working gut. Some parents have reported successes in reducing the symptoms of autism in their child when following a biomedical programme.

If you consider trying biomedical intervention, you must seek professional advice. Biomedical treatment is not currently recognized as mainstream medical practice and is not available on the NHS.

So, many therapies are dependent on others in order to produce the best results. Just treating your child's gut is not enough if you do not then fully utilize your child's increased potential to learn. You will need to support their enhanced ability with other learning therapies, such as an ABA programme.

Education and the EHCP Process

At some point you will probably need to apply for additional help for your child. This may well be before your child even commences in a nursery or school setting. The earlier you start any form of extra help or therapy, the better the outcome for your child.

SEN Support at School

If your child has been identified as having some problems at school, he or she may receive special educational needs (SEN) support. All schools should have a clear approach to identifying and responding to SEN. Mainstream schools should publish their SEN arrangements, and these should be available to be read on their school website. Further details should also be found in your local authority's Local Offer.

This may mean that your child may need some additional hours of support within a nursery placement or school setting. They may need help in many different ways, perhaps placing them in a quieter area to learn or to encourage certain skills. An Individual Education Plan (IEP) may be formulated by the school, but as a parent you should also be involved in the discussion about what is included in this IEP. The IEP is a planning, teaching and reviewing tool, and should set out three or four precise goals or targets within time frames. These short-term targets and strategies for your child should be different from, or in addition to, those in place for the rest of the class and should be reviewed on a regular basis. As an alternative to an IEP, some schools now use provision mapping, which outlines the provision that the school can provide.

Your child with autism will almost certainly need specialist additional help from a speech and language therapist (SLT) and most likely from an occupational therapist (OT), too.

All schools and nurseries will have a designated Special Educational Needs Coordinator (SENCO). Your child may need additional hours of one-to-one support on an individual basis, or to be placed in a small group of children who may have similar needs. The group may have specialist support, or your child may have one-to-one support within the group. Your child should have an individualized programme, which means that they should have the appropriate support for their own needs. They may need a combination of support. For example, if they have speech delay, they may require some one-to-one intensive speech therapy sessions; additionally, they may also attend a small speech and language therapy group, which may be within the nursery or school setting or even outside of it. For example, if your child is reluctant to speak up in class, the IEP may have a clause so that the teacher is reminded to prompt your child with a question on a regular basis to encourage participation.

The level of support needed by children with autism can vary enormously, hence the different levels of support available. If you have a very inclusive school with good SEN practice (and provision), then you may get the support your child needs without having to fight too hard to get it. If, however, you feel your child needs more support than they are receiving, then you need to be prepared to battle on their behalf to get as much help as you feel your child requires.

In reality, most children with an early diagnosis of ASD will require more support than a school can offer without an education, health and care (EHCP) plan in place. You will most likely have to apply for an EHCP for your child before they can even start to attend nursery or school in order for some support to be put into place prior to them starting. As EHCP plans can be applied for from birth, this means that if your child has obvious and severe difficulties you can apply for an EHCP plan as early as you need to.

In the past, a child was given a statement of SEN and the process you went through in order to get extra educational help was known as 'statementing'. Although statements have now been replaced by a new system called EHCPs, many people will probably still refer to this as going through the 'statementing' process.

In September 2014, the Special Educational Needs and Disability (SEND) reforms were fully implemented to phase in the new EHCP plans. Statements used to be issued to children between the ages of two and nineteen and were solely for the purpose of SEN. The new EHCP plans can be issued from birth until the age of twenty-five. All existing statements are still valid and the LAs have until April 2018 to transfer all existing statements to EHCP plans.

Education, Health and Care Plan (EHCP)

The old system of issuing a statement has been phased out and SENs are now included in the EHCP process that encompasses SEN and health and social care needs. The government has decided that each LA can decide their own format for an EHCP, but the government still maintains control over the content so the EHCP has to include the same categories. There are several parts in the EHCP listed from A to K. For educational needs, the specific sections are part B (the special educational needs), part F (special educational provision) and part I (school placement).

For those children with severe and complex education and health care needs, this plan should bring together all aspects of care they require. For example, your child may have a physical disability and require an educational setting that can meet both their SEN and their physical ones. There may be a cross-over between social needs and educational ones in a child with severe behavioural issues. If the behaviours are not being managed correctly, then it will be almost impossible to try to educate a child in the normal way.

The Local Offer

The Children and Families Act 2014 placed a statutory duty on each LA to develop and publish its Local Offer. This Local Offer is individual to each LA and puts together information about the availability of education, health and care services, plus leisure activities and support groups, for local children with disabilities and SEN in that area. Each LA's Local Offer should be easily accessible on the internet. Online you should also be able to find information on SEN provision within local schools and what type of specialist schools are available in your area.

The Local Offer is intended to make information easily available to help you make an informed choice so that you can be actively involved in the educational decisions for your child.

Requesting and Obtaining an EHCP

For the purpose of getting educational help for your child, the process of requesting and obtaining an EHCP is similar to the old process of getting a statement in place. Going through the EHCP process can be one of the hardest things you need to do as the parent of a child with special needs. It can be a very demanding, stressful time and emotionally exhausting. It is also a lengthy process and will probably take a minimum of six months from start to finish before you get the final EHCP. If you do not accept the final EHCP and end up fighting to change it at the Special Educational Needs and Disability (SEND) Tribunal, the process could take up to a further year. Meanwhile, you may be paying for any additional support you feel your child needs, but which is not addressed by the EHCP you have been offered. So the process can be very drawn out and very costly in term of your finances and emotions.

The actual process of applying for an EHCP takes approximately twenty weeks. When you put in a request for an EHCP, your LA has six weeks in which to decide whether to go ahead with a full assessment. In this initial six weeks, your LA should seek appropriate advice and information from varying professionals. If it decides not to go ahead with the full assessment, you have the right to appeal against this decision. The whole process of EHC assessment and developing the EHCP, from the point at which the assessment is requested until the final EHCP is issued, must take no longer than twenty weeks (subject to exemptions). If any exemptions apply, you should be informed of this.

Your LA will seek advice and information about your child from you as the parent, from someone such as a head teacher from an educational setting (if your child is already in one), medical advice from a health care professional, psychological advice from an educational psychologist and from social services in relation to social care.

Your child will have to be assessed by a variety of professionals and the reports they write can be distressing to read. In the best interests of your child, the reports must state bald facts and the needs of your child while being devoid of any emotion. It sounds quite strange to say but in time you will be grateful for a report that paints your child's difficulties in the worst light as this will help to increase the amount of support you are offered. It is, of course, necessary for professionals to focus on your child's weaknesses as well as their strengths. All the reports are intended to help your child receive the highest level of support possible.

I would receive a report that would make me cry as I read it. On paper, my beautiful boy sounded so severe and so hopeless. No mention of his affectionate nature or his lovely smile. But, through my tears, I would smile and silently thank the writer for a report that would help me in the fight to get what my son needed.

The new system of EHCPs now focuses more positively on what a child can do and what they have achieved as well as what they are unable to do and need support with. So your child's EHCP and other reports should now mention both the positives and the negatives.

However it is disguised, for example, labelling a child with global developmental delay as opposed to labelling them with having severe learning difficulties, you will be reminded that this label is actually being applied to your precious child. Your child most probably will have been born perfect and only recently have begun to lose skills such as eye contact. You may only have been aware for a short time that your child is no longer gaining expected skills such as speech. Most likely you will still be in a state of grief, shock or, for some people, denial about your child's condition or expectations. Coming to terms with your child's diagnosis and then almost immediately being expected to put into place all that your child needs, is an enormous emotional undertaking for you as a parent. For some people, taking action may form part of their own healing process, and taking on the project that is now your child's development may keep you so busy that you have little time to dwell on anything else.

During this process, you may want to request a certain nursery or school placement, or perhaps a different form of education. You can also request that a LA considers making a direct payment to you instead of special educational provision, so you can then spend this on education yourself. This is known as a *personal budget* and information about the availability of personal budgets should be found within each LA's Local Offer.

You will receive a draft EHCP once all the assessments have taken place, and you will have fifteen days to consider the plan and respond to it. Once the twenty weeks' time limit is reached, you should receive the final EHCP. Ideally, it will contain everything you have requested, but if your LA is not in agreement with your wishes for your child, you may then have to start an appeal process to try to get what you do want. If, for example, you have decided upon a therapy such as ABA for your child, it is unlikely that your LA will agree to this. Be warned: appealing to a SEND tribunal can be a very expensive, time-consuming and emotionally draining process.

We had three costly tribunals for three of my boys to get the ABA therapy I felt they needed. Although it cost us a great deal in monetary terms as well as stress, I still feel absolutely convinced that my boys needed this therapy. Fortunately, the tribunal panels agreed in our favour. However, we still had to pay for all the therapy during the process as well as the legal costs, which are not normally refundable.

Getting the Right Educational Help

Beware of those who tell you that autism is a lifelong condition and that because there is nothing you can do about it, you should just get on with it and accept your child's diagnosis. Autism is one condition where there is a great deal you *can* do. Admittedly, you may not be able to 'cure' your child, but you can make a huge difference to their quality of life. Getting the right kind of educational support is one of the most important things that you can do for your child. Hope is a crucial part of your child's future.

The use of the term 'delay' implies exactly that: that your child is simply delayed and will, by assumption, be able to 'catch up'. Perhaps a child who is delayed in walking will start to walk a little later in life than other children, but in the end they will walk perfectly normally. A few years later, there will be nothing to indicate that there was ever a delay with walking and nothing to distinguish them from other children. Unfortunately, a diagnosis of delayed speech in autism is not very helpful. It can mean a minor delay or a very serious one in which your child may never acquire a normal level of speech. The term 'delay' is probably used because in autism it is very difficult to predict how each child will progress. At age three, if a child has no language, it is hard to predict whether they will acquire normal language in later years.

One of my boys at three just hummed and could not understand or speak any language at all. He was labelled as being on the severe end of the autistic spectrum because of this. With huge amounts of intensive therapy and support, he is now fully conversational and although he does not converse at the same level as a child his age, he would now be labelled as having high-functioning autism.

A more accurate prediction of future ability can be made at around the age of five. If your child is still non-verbal at age five, then the likelihood of acquiring normal speech would be much lower than it might have been at three. Even so, this is still just an educated guess, and some children have been known to start speaking later than the age of five and do very well. The lesson is: never give up hope and accept what you have been told as an absolute.

Professionals tend to paint a gloomier picture than parents do. Having said that, it would be far worse if you were told that your child would 'recover' in the future and you held onto false expectations while your child did not improve as much as you expected. Your disappointment and sorrow would probably be worse than the original diagnosis of autism. Giving false hope is not fair to anyone. It is perhaps better that your child's prognosis is unpredictable and, if you achieve much more for your child than was expected, you will of course be delighted and very proud. The outcomes for a child who has an early diagnosis of ASD cannot be precisely predicted and measured. In some ways, this is what keeps parents fighting for their children every step of the way – somehow the fact that you really do not know what your child may be capable of achieving keeps you going.

So you will need to get the best help for your child as soon as you can. The earlier you start therapy and education for your child, the better their outcome will be. You may wish that someone else would come along and sort it all for you, but only you really know your child and what is best for them. If you rely on the authorities and professionals to tell you what your child needs and what is best for them, you may end up with the minimum support that they are obliged to offer. You may also not end up with the most appropriate support for your child.

Choosing a School or Nursery

There are many choices to be made, such as opting for mainstream education or special needs schools and nurseries. There may be choices later on as your child gets older when you may have to choose between a residential school or keeping your child at home and sending them to school in the daytime. There is no direct path for any child on the autistic spectrum and along the way you as a parent are entitled to make choices and decisions about your child's education. Obviously, you will seek guidance on the choices that you make, and this guidance may come from other parents or from specialists.

Just looking at schools or nurseries can be an exhausting process on its own (and sometimes, sadly, a disappointing one). A visit may entail a lengthy discussion about your child's needs and perhaps an assessment involving your child. Although all mainstream schools are legally obliged to accept children with SEN, there is a vast difference between a school that actively welcomes children with special needs and one that accepts them because it must.

At nursery level, there are many private nurseries that will take state funding, so you may need to make a choice between a private nursery and a state-maintained nursery that may or may not be attached to a primary school. Even at nursery level, there are many differences in how a nursery is run. There are Montessori nurseries and others that expect a child to achieve certain academic goals in numeracy and literacy before they leave to go to primary school. Some nurseries place a greater emphasis on play or the arts.

Nurseries can also vary in size, so you might find a large nursery with extensive facilities and many children attending it, or a smaller nursery, perhaps based in someone's house, with fewer children. Depending on how your child is able to interact with other children, or whether they have sensory issues, you may need to consider the environment within the nursery quite carefully.

Mainstream or Special Needs?

There are also a limited number of special needs nurseries or even autism-specific nurseries. From a very early age, you may need to make an initial choice or decision about whether you wish your child to be educated in a mainstream setting or a special needs one. There may be an obvious choice depending on the severity of your child's autism at that time or the issues that they have. If not, there are different arguments for and against both options.

A child with autism may be non-verbal and so would therefore seem to be better placed in a special needs environment, however they may be able to cope in a noisy, mainstream environment and gain some valuable social skills while there. Later on, if the child is having difficulty in accessing mainstream education, they may then move to a special needs school. On the other hand, another child may be fully verbal and able to communicate, which would imply that they should be in a mainstream setting, yet they may have severe sensory issues and find a mainstream setting overwhelming. It may be therefore that the child who appears to be higher functioning is the one who most needs to be in a special needs environment at that time. So, choices need to be made about where that child would most benefit from being at that point in time. Currently, in order to get a high level of educational support for your child, you will need to apply for an EHCP (*see* page 169), although a nursery may be able to provide a low level of support if this is all your child requires.

Do not confuse your child's educational needs with care needs. If you need respite care or help to share the care needs of your child, then you need to request help from social services or charities. Educational provision will not provide your child with a babysitter or carer so that you can get on with all the things in your life that you need to function well. If you need help in order to be able to carry on working, then you need a package of support from social services or other agencies. This should be included in the EHCP, but will be separate from the educational provision and should be negotiated separately. Be mindful of this when you ask for help from the educational department. The only exception may be if your child has severe and complex needs and so may need a specialist residential setting that can meet all their varying needs.

Midway during one of our SEND tribunal hearings, our local authority hastily tried to put together a list of possible nurseries to support my children in the afternoons as it was only offering a limited number of hours at a specialist nursery. I was fighting for a full-time ABA programme that would provide the educational support needed by my boys. I answered that I wasn't looking for childcare in the afternoons: my boys needed education, not babysitting. We were awarded the full hours of an ABA programme that we had asked for.

You will need to be very clear about your expectations and do your own research into what is available and what you feel would be best to support your child. You can ring up nurseries and ask to visit and meet with the staff. Try to talk with other parents in your area to see what is on offer, whether state-funded or privately funded. Unfortunately, your LA is not obliged to offer the best that is available at any price, as it does have budgets to manage. Your job is to get the best provision you can for your child while the job of your LA is to keep costs down. You will not therefore be able to get everything that is available that your child could benefit from; there would not in any event be enough hours in your child's day to do that. You need to prioritize and decide what would have the most beneficial effect and what is reasonable to expect. You should be able to find out what other parents have managed to get onto their child's statement or EHCP, and that should be your minimum aim. Also bear in mind that the needs of all children are individual, so one child may have been awarded a higher level of support than another because their needs are greater. This is particularly pertinent in the case of a diagnosis of ASD as the needs of a child can vary so enormously. The spectrum is a very wide, all-encompassing label and can be applied to those children who will be able to lead an independent life and who have normal language as well as those who will be dependent on full-time care for the rest of their lives. Therefore, it is your child's needs that are the most important factor to consider when applying for an EHCP, and not your child's diagnosis.

7

KEEP CALM AND CARRY ON

So, AFTER A DIAGNOSIS of autism, how do you pick up the pieces and carry on with your life? *Can* you carry on with your life as before? Unfortunately not. Becoming a parent alters your life enormously from the day your first child is born. If your child is then given a diagnosis of autism, your life and the lives of those around you are changed again.

Acceptance
One of the hardest aspects of dealing with your child being given a diagnosis of autism is acceptance, both of your child's condition and perhaps of your child, also. You will have loved your child from birth, or from when they first came to you, and you will not have had any idea of what was to come. Although the diagnosis will probably be a huge shock to you, the hidden blessing will be that you already know and love your child for who he or she is. You will have already had precious time to bond and so you will be more prepared to take on whatever life throws at you and your child.

So, although autism is absolutely not what you were hoping and expecting for your child's future, by the time you realize that your child has a disability, you will already love them unconditionally. Would it help if you knew their possible diagnosis pre-birth? Perhaps. And perhaps in the future it will be possible to predict those babies who may potentially go on to develop autism. There is already early research showing there may be some chemical changes during pregnancy to indicate possible autism, but as there is still no definitive medical test to diagnose actual autism, this is not currently of any real help. Being forewarned might mean that your child was given the earliest possible help and that you could start any treatment or therapy at a very early age. It is well known that the younger the age the child is when you start intervention, the better the outcome for that child. You might also not have to fight for everything your child needs if you had a diagnosis at birth.

A friend with a child born with Down's syndrome said it was a huge shock when her daughter was born with Down's syndrome as she had no warning at all. A little later on, though, she did say that, unlike autism, because her child had a known disability she was given help and support from birth. The authorities can't argue with a proven condition.

Does autism exist from birth? Research is still at an early stage to try to define what autism actually is, and whether it is genetic and inevitable, or whether it is genetic but triggered by one of a number of factors. Or indeed, is it genetic at all? There are too many potential ideas about this to try to form an opinion at the moment. If autism is a medical condition, then are our children pre-disposed to developing autism or do they already have the condition before they are born? If they are pre-disposed to it, then is there anything we can do to prevent it from happening? Does that mean that autism is a time bomb waiting in the wings and, if so, what is the trigger? Are there many different triggers? Along with parents of children with many other medical conditions such as diabetes there are many unanswered questions. Although diabetes is a very different example, it also seems to suddenly develop in children with no other history and research is currently underway to try and find the cause or trigger in these children.

So, if you had the knowledge before your baby was even born that they might already have or develop autism in the future would that help or hinder your relationship with your baby? We know that a very high proportion of parents with babies diagnosed with Down's syndrome in the first trimester choose to terminate their pregnancies as those parents feel they will be unable to cope with a disabled child. Would the parents of a potentially autistic child feel the same way? Or would society pressure them to feel this way? If there was more acceptance and support in society for children with disabilities, would this change the way that people feel about having a child with a disability? There is no measure or scoring system to predict the potential severity of autism in any child, so would a pre-natal diagnosis help? It might give you time to come to terms with a possible diagnosis, but as the diagnosis would be so vague and uncertain this could potentially be more frightening than the reality turns out to be. There is no way of predicting how severe a child's autism may turn out to be.

I was grateful not to have a diagnosis for my fourth son for the first two years of his life. I wanted to just enjoy him for who he was and stay in my bubble of hope that he would be fine. Although the risk of him also being autistic like his older three brothers was very high, I didn't want to dwell on this and spend every moment thinking about it and watching for signs. I am sure other people did, the most hurtful being children at his older brothers' primary school who met him at only a few days old and asked me if he was autistic, too. At the time of his birth, he wasn't autistic to my knowledge and I was determined to keep that thought at bay for a while.

Moving Forwards Post-Diagnosis

Once you do have a diagnosis you need to try to get on with your life now knowing that you have a disabled child and all the responsibility this will entail for the rest of your life and theirs. All of your children will always be a defining part of your life. Children without disabilities grow up and lead independent lives of their own in which you may still play a large part but you usually no longer have responsibility for them. Children with disabilities will remain your responsibility forever, and this realization can feel overwhelming at the beginning.

That feeling of being overwhelmed will come and go and change as time goes on and your children grow up, but it will become something you live with. Even if you make a decision for your child at some stage to move into residential care, although you may no longer have the day-to-day responsibility for your child, you will still have overall responsibility as a parent and will need to make important decisions about your child's future. Autism parents are often known as 'warrior Mums or Dads' who will fight the world for their child. Of course, most parents will fight for what they believe is right for their children, but parents of a child with autism will have to fight harder for a condition that is still not totally understood or, more importantly, fully supported by society.

Family Life and Siblings

How do you juggle your family life with other children you may have? How will your child with autism affect their lives? Again, some of this will depend on the severity of your child's autism and how they develop as they grow up. How do you try to do the best you can for all your children? Any child with a disability will command much of your attention and time because of their issues and needs. You may find it is a full-time job caring for one child with autism, let alone having other siblings to look after at the same time.

Sometimes, as in the case of my family, you may have more than one child with autism to look after, and that will put an even bigger strain on your capacity to cope and do the best you can for each child.

It is unfair on another child to expect them unconditionally to take on any of the care for a sibling with a disability, but most of them do, without question or judgement. They will often love and care for their sibling in the way that you do. Perhaps a child who is without the preconceived ideas and prejudice about disability that most adults have is in a better position of acceptance than most adults are. Children are very accepting of others, which you will also find later on when your child starts nursery or school. It is usually their parents who instil fear or prejudice in them. The difficult part is being able to separate your individual children's lives and endeavouring not to let a sibling's disability impact in a negative way on the lives of your other children.

Growing up with a sibling with a disability can be enriching for a sibling. They will learn tolerance and acceptance of others from a very early age and the experience will probably help them to develop into caring and thoughtful individuals. But as children they too are entitled to as normal a life as possible and to achieve as much in their lives as they can. This will probably mean that you will need some extra help. Otherwise, your time and energy will be severely stretched trying to do your best for everyone.

Juggling Finances

How do you juggle finances to ensure that it is fair on *all* your children? Having a child with autism can be very expensive in terms of having to provide all the therapies that will enhance their development but which unfortunately may often need to be paid for by you because of a lack of funding in the health or education or social services departments. In an ideal world, any resources or therapy needed would be provided by the social and educational systems, but funds are limited and so parents often end up paying for vital services themselves. How do you manage to provide everything you wish your special needs child to have at the same time as providing everything you feel your other children should also have? This is where you need all the financial help that you can get for your child with autism in order to make sure that they get the most you can provide for them.

You do not want to cause resentment among your children by providing more time and more resources for your special needs child than for their siblings. In any family, it is hard to treat all your children fairly and equally, but what if you had a gifted child or one who excelled at sport? Families of future Olympians must have sacrificed and put one child's needs above the others due to exceptional circumstances. Your child with autism is exceptional, too, and needs as much time and energy as you can provide. You may have to share some of the care of your children among relatives and friends and accept that you cannot do it all yourself.

Your own children may happily and willingly want to help care for their sibling with special needs. If they want to be involved, then that is wonderful for you and your family. If they do not, then it would be unfair to expect them.

Although there is a nine-year age gap between my oldest and my youngest son, there is a very special bond. My oldest is also autistic so perhaps he understands his little brother better because of this, but he has loved him unconditionally since the day he was born. He takes baths with him, plays with him and looks after him as best he can. My other sons accept their little brother as a slightly annoying little person who wrecks their Lego models, and I would not expect them to help look after him.

Separate Bedrooms

If you can, try to keep your other children from having to share a bedroom with a sibling with autism. A child with autism may have problems getting to sleep, staying asleep, gaining continence skills as well as other issues. Your other children need a proper night's sleep, so if sleep is an issue you will need to keep them separate. Your ASD child may pull things out of cupboards and generally make a mess of their rooms. It is unfair on a sibling to have to cope with this and a sibling will probably need space of their own to retreat to for peace and quiet from time to time.

I have locks on the outsides of my other boys' bedroom doors so that we can lock their rooms to prevent the littlest one getting in and trashing all their stuff while they are at school. If they come home and find their rooms and things in a mess or broken, how can I expect them to be pleased to see their little brother?

Siblings of Special Needs Children

As your children get older, you may find that there are activities for siblings of children with special needs where they can meet other children in a similar position. There may be support groups and counselling available, if you think they need it. It may be helpful for children to meet other children who may also have assumed the role of a carer. If your child with autism is quite passive and does not greatly alter your normal family life, you may find that your other children accept their sibling's differences with few problems. But it is more likely that your child will not be passive, and will create noise and chaos so your other children will need to learn how to handle this. They may become very protective of their sibling with special needs. It is usually adults who have issues around the acceptance of differences and not children. If your children grow up with a brother or sister with special needs, they are more likely to grow up without prejudice or any preconceived ideas of how life should be lived. Your other children will learn a life-enhancing lesson and will hopefully spread the message to others around them.

We have a fabulous part-time babysitter who has two younger brothers on the autistic spectrum. She has grown up with autism and now chooses to work with our boys because of this. She could work in any

---

other field or babysit for children without special needs, but she really enjoys being with our boys. She is proof that living with autism can be so rewarding that you choose more of it.

You should not be defined by being the parent of a special needs child, although it is often the case. In the same way, your other children should not be defined by being part of a special needs family. Hopefully, your other children will benefit as much from your special needs child as he or she will benefit from having siblings who love and accept them for who they are. Other children make great role models (when their behaviour is good!), so you will have teachers on hand without them knowing it! An adult can get on the floor and pretend to play with trains, but it is so much better for a child to learn naturally from another child who is genuinely playing. Imitation is a key skill to acquire in order to learn other skills in the future and once a child has learned to imitate, you can teach them so much more. After all, speech is learned by listening and copying, so imitation is a fundamental skill.

There might be more difficult scenarios, though, if you have a child who has severe temper tantrums or can be aggressive towards other children. Sadly, because of their own problems, some children with autism can become very frustrated and may physically hurt other adults or children. Sometimes it may be their only real method of communication. You will need to ensure that your other children are not subjected to any violence. Rough play, even physical fighting is normal amongst siblings, but even then they generally do not cause much harm or any real injury. This may mean that you cannot leave your ASD child in a room with other children without a responsible adult being present.

I had a situation for the first two years of my youngest child's life where he could not be left in the same room as one of my other older boys. He didn't mean to harm anyone intentionally, but he had no idea that a baby was not a toy and could have seriously injured him if they were left together in the same room. This meant I had to take my youngest son with me wherever I went in the house to guarantee his safety.

Adapting Family Life
Trying to have a normal family life can be very trying indeed!

185

If your child with autism needs to watch a film at a special needs screening, does that mean you expect your other children to attend the same screening? Will the noise and possible disruptions spoil their enjoyment of an outing? But do you have the time and energy and resources to take them to separate cinema screenings? Will your other children mature at different rates, meaning that a younger sibling may outgrow an activity before their older, affected brother or sister? It can be hard with age differences trying to accommodate everyone in a family, but if you add special needs and different ages of maturity to the equation, the task can become harder still to juggle.

Sometimes there are small advantages in having a brother or sister with special needs. For example, at a theme park like Legoland, children with autism are given special exit permits so they do not have to queue for each ride. You are allowed a small number of guests to accompany them each time, so your other children or friends can also skip the queues. When going on holiday, you should be allowed to jump queues at the check-in desk at airports and, hopefully, choose where you sit on the plane.

However, you may come across resentment from other parents who have been standing in a queue and who demand to know why they have to wait in a line and you don't. I was saddened by one very irate family who were complaining about the entry fee they had paid and how unfair it was after having paid all that money that they still had to queue when we didn't. I would happily have paid their entry fee a thousand times over to have a 'normal' family like they had. You may be able to sell the positives to your own children, but in reality we would love to be able to queue like everyone else if it meant our children were also like everyone else's, i.e. without the addition of the negative parts of autism in their lives.

Giving Up Work

You may have to adapt family life in many ways. In the early years, you may have to put a great deal of your life as you know it on hold. You may decide you have to give up work as you may find it almost impossible to work and to look after a special needs child. Your child may need watching and taking care of every minute of every day. Of course, all children need care and attention, but most children are able to entertain themselves for short periods of time, and certainly after a few years, children begin to understand rules about what they can and cannot do. Your child with autism may not be able to behave in an age-appropriate way or have any idea at all about safety or rules. You may find that they need someone with them constantly and you may not have time to do simple household tasks, let alone contemplate working in any official capacity. Even if you find a nanny or carer who is able to look after your child while you work, you may still find that you do not have the energy to work as your child may have disturbed sleep patterns, which means you in turn will have disturbed nights.

Additional Workload in Having a Child with Special Needs

You will also have extra administration, paperwork and appoint-ments to take your child to, and these can take up a great deal of your time. You cannot expect a nanny or carer to take your child to important appointments and assessments where the professionals will expect at least one parent to be present. You may have a very understanding workplace or are self-employed, but the additional expectations on a special needs parent are great and you may end up being torn in two trying to meet everyone's needs. You will also need to have 100 per cent reliable childcare, or you will end up taking days off work every time your carer takes a day off.

At this point, I should emphasize not being able to work means giving up 'paid work' as looking after a special needs child is more than a full-time job! Some mornings you may find yourself longing to go off to a paid job just to give yourself a break!

Loss of Finances

Another downside of not working for money may mean financially juggling with the loss of a salary. With that may also come a loss of financial independence for whichever parent decides to give up work. You also need to consider that not only are you potentially giving up one salary, but that you will spend more on bringing up your child than you would do on a child without a disability so it can be a double blow that you have to give up earning money at a time when you could actually do with more. So you may go from a partnership where both of you work to one where one partner works and the other is at home, essentially doing an extreme form of childcare. With pre-school-age children, it is normal to have to either pay for childcare or to look after your children yourself in an unpaid role as their mother or father. When your children are at school age and you are still in the position of needing full-time childcare, the financial implications can be huge.

My twins as teenagers still need looking after every hour of every day, which means carers or babysitters are needed for them if I am not free. One irony of them needing babysitters is that other teenagers of the same age are themselves starting to earn pocket money babysitting for younger children. So, not only have we missed out on a stage where we don't need to pay babysitters anymore, but our children have also fallen behind yet another stage and remain fully dependent on us.

Maintaining Your Identity

Along with the financial loss of a salary or your previous way of life, you also need to consider your own identity and what you may be able to do to try to preserve it. In reality, this is very, very hard. People may wrongly presume that you are sitting around at home all day drinking coffee. When someone asks 'What do you do?' and you no longer have a job to be defined by, you will have to reply that you are at home as a full-time carer. Often, trying to explain what that actually entails to someone who does not have a special needs child is not always easy. More thoughtful people may think to enquire what you may have done in your 'past life', i.e. the one before you had children, and perhaps respect you for having made the decision to stay at home to care for your child. Again, having a special needs child is a great social leveller: we are all carers and cleaners once we no longer 'work'. Sometimes, though, you may find yourself wanting to say that you are not *just* a carer and that you used to be someone with a totally different label. Perhaps retired people also suffer from the same loss of identity when they have to give their working situation as being 'retired' rather than using the working title by which they were probably known for years. Society seems to have diminished the role of stay-at-home Mums and Dads in an era where everyone is expected to have some form of career.

Considering Your Own Needs

As a mother or father, considering your own needs above your child's is something that many find quite hard to do. It is instinctive to put our children first. Unfortunately, many, many parents of children with disabilities become burned out from the stress caused by the physical and mental caring for their child. So, if you feel guilty considering yourself, remember: if you crash, your child will have no one to care for them. So never feel guilty.

But how can you justify spending money or time on yourself when your money is often desperately needed for other things? How do you weigh up the cost of an hour of therapy for yourself when you could be spending that money on an hour of therapy for your child? The long-term effect of your child having as much therapy as you can afford may mean in the future that your life will be made easier. They may need less care ultimately because of all the therapy you have paid for. The short- and long-term effects of depriving yourself of any necessary therapy could, however, mean that you become stressed and ill and unable to care for your child, and this can become a vicious cycle. If no one else is kind enough to make sure you have time for yourself and your needs, then you will have to learn to be kind to yourself.

Many of us parents have learned this the hard way after years of not caring for or looking after ourselves. I wish I had had a mother who might have been there to look after me a little at times and prevent the damage I have inadvertently done to myself after so many years of full-time caring. It is not selfish to consider yourself and to give yourself a break, but it often feels self-indulgent and so we don't do it often enough.

You may need some counselling or therapy to come to terms with your child's diagnosis. Some people never actually get to a point of real acceptance. Perhaps that can be a positive as it means you will keep fighting to try to change and enhance your child's life and future. However, if you cannot live with the fact that your child has a lifelong disorder and are continually distressed and depressed about it, your life will be so much harder than it could be. We do not need to be 'Pollyanna'-like and joyful about autism, but we do need to get ourselves into a place where we can get through each day and appreciate the positives in our lives, including our much-loved children.

If one parent is more accepting than the other of their child's disability, this can be very difficult for a relationship. Grandparents, too, may not be accepting and may come out with platitudes saying that your child 'will grow out of it'. If they come from a previous generation where the word 'autism' was not widely used or known about, it can be hard for them to understand that it is a real condition that will not just go away. There is so much you can do once you are able to confront your child's diagnosis, believe it, accept it as far as you are able, and then move on into loving and caring for your child. It is very hard to be positive for your child if you remain in a state of disbelief and so you should seek help at an early stage if you feel permanently down all the time. It is not weakness to accept that you need help, nor is it a rejection of your child if you feel overwhelmed by caring for them.

Coping with the Stress

If you are able to come to terms with the diagnosis, but feel stressed by the whole situation, you may want to try complementary forms of stress relief like massage or reflexology. Most of all you will need time off away from your child to be able to function alone as yourself and be seen not just as a special needs parent.

So what can you do for yourself to keep calm and be able to carry on? It is very important to remember that you as a parent are usually the anchor that keeps everything together. You will be responsible for many peoples' lives as well as your own. Yes, this would be true of any parent, but is especially true of a parent in your situation. A parent of a child with special needs has such additional responsibility and a great deal more looking after to do in order to keep the family functioning (or, indeed, flourishing). Unfortunately, you will encounter many people who just do not see, or do not wish to see, the difference having a child with special needs makes to your life. Ignore those people observing and not understanding how much additional effort you are having to make. Your child may look to outward appearances exactly like other children with no issues. There may be no obvious physical features or differences so you may find little support from some people.

If people do not understand the strain you may be under and the physical demands that are being made upon you, then they will probably not consider the fact that you might need a break or support from them. After all, they too may have children and their attitude may be that childcare is tiring, but we all do it, so why do you need extra help? The luckiest families have supportive grandparents/parents/siblings or wider extended family willing and able to step in and offer support. For those to whom this applies, hopefully this unconditional support will be enough to sustain you. Having good family support can mean so much. It may come in the form of additional childcare for your child with autism, or childcare for your other children. Even more importantly, sometimes, it will mean emotional support for you. Having someone willing to listen, to understand, not to judge and to support you is priceless. You cannot buy or pay for love and support that is unconditional and available when you most need it. Some people will have families who offer both practical and emotional support and, hopefully, will not need to seek out support elsewhere. If you do not have a supportive family (sadly, all too common), then you will have to find the time and energy to seek out that help and support. Of course, the whole point is that you do not have the time and energy, so how are you going to get the support you need, both physically and emotionally?

Emotional Support

If you are older parents, your own parents may be unable to help. Indeed, inevitably they will be older, and they may even be at a stage of needing your help and support. Not only will you not get any support from them, but you may also be expected to be there to support them. Your own family members such as your siblings may be too busy getting on with their own lives to support you in theirs. People are sometimes supportive in the early acute stages of a life-changing situation, such as a sudden illness, bereavement or change in circumstances. After a while, though, you may find that the support drops off and your problems become commonplace and part of the fabric of life to other people, but obviously not to you. So you may find a rush of support and help when your child is first diagnosed, but then this support and help fading away in time. Of course, with time your energy is increasingly depleted and while emotionally you may be dealing better with your child's diagnosis, as time goes on, your physical energy will also decrease. You may also find the mental stress of looking after your child increasingly tiring as you continually fight for what your child needs and deserves. So just when people start to think that you are no longer need their support, you may actually be needing it more ...

Long-Term Tiredness

A mother with a newborn baby may complain of tiredness and of being woken during the night, but eventually this situation will improve and there will come a time when her baby begins to sleep through the night, and once more she will have enough sleep. This is a temporary circumstance, which is, of course, quite normal and your hormones and happiness at having a new baby will hopefully see most people through this stage. A parent with a child with autism who has a sleep disorder may never get consistent sleep for years on end. Sleep deprivation on a long-term permanent basis can have a profound effect on the parent looking after that child. These are the hidden effects that others do not observe because they do not live your life. It is well known that sleep deprivation can affect your health, your ability to make sound judgements and, of course, your mental state. If you have a child who regularly wakes during the night, then you need practical support in the form of a night off from time to time, or respite care in the form perhaps of an overnight carer to stay with your child so that you can get a proper night's sleep. Even with some respite, the long-term strain of never having enough sleep can have serious consequences on health.

Even if you are at home full time and not working in any official category, you will still need some help with childcare in order to be able to make all the phone calls, write reports, attend appointments and all the other things that take up so much of your time. Managing all the paperwork and filling in forms can be very time-consuming on top of looking after a child you cannot leave alone on their own for a minute.

I have a filing cabinet full of paperwork, ordered in categorized sections for medical reports, biomedical results and reports, speech and language and other therapies, all the paperwork leading to statements of SEN, including all the legal documentation, annual reviews, social services and direct payments – and then all the ABA paperwork and files. In my case, I have this administration to the power of four as all four of my boys have autism. This is just the extra paperwork because of their autism and is on top of all the other paperwork usually needed for any child as regards to schooling, after-school clubs and hobbies. Some mothers have been known to carry paperwork around in a wheelie suitcase to meetings instead of a briefcase!

Family Holidays

Having a family holiday may be a wonderful idea in theory, but holidaying with a child with autism can be less of a holiday than staying at home might be. But everyone needs a break and you need to feel as much like a normal family as you can, so this means having holidays like everyone else. Whoever coined the phrase 'A change is as good as a rest' was certainly not a parent with a special needs child, as a change of routine may be good for many of us, but for a child with autism, change can be one of the hardest things to deal with.

A very few fortunate families will have sufficient income to be able to deal more easily with the problems of a family holiday entailing other children or, indeed, enabling the parents to have a break, too. If finances allow, you might be able to take along some additional one-to-one support specifically to look after your child with autism. The downside to this will mean having to budget for an additional wage, an extra bedroom or hotel room, probably an extra flight or train seat. Also, it will also mean that your family holiday will not just involve you and your children, but also a non-family member who will be with you for a lot of the time.

To avoid this, perhaps a grandparent or other supportive member of your extended family could accompany you, instead? This would at least mean that your family holiday is as close to being a 'family' holiday as you can manage. Many families go on holiday anyway with grandparents or cousins, so if you have supportive ones you are in the lucky minority and should be able to enjoy a proper family holiday, and even get a bit of a break yourself.

Another alternative is to book an organized family holiday with activities where some one-to-one childcare can be arranged at your destination. There are some family holiday companies that offer childcare clubs or specifically one-to-one childcare for special needs children at their ski or beach resorts. It is always worth approaching a company directly and enquiring if it can accommodate and look after your child. Of course, this means that your child will need to be able to adapt to a new environment and a carer unfamiliar to them while remaining happy and safe. If you do not think that your child can be looked after by someone they do not know, then you will have to take your own childcare with you. You may find that booking a private house or villa is a better option than a resort if your child has behaviours that are quite hard to manage and they might find the presence of too many strangers overwhelming. Safety can be an important consideration while on holiday. You may be able to leave your child in another room for short periods of time at home, for example, if they are playing happily or watching a film while you are cooking, but on holiday in an unknown and potentially dangerous environment, you may need to have someone with them for twenty-four hours a day. Your home may be childproof, but a holiday home or hotel room is probably not.

Travelling

You will most likely have to adapt where you go depending on your child's needs. The practicalities of travel are the first things to consider. A child who gets up and runs off is not a good candidate for a train journey. There are no safety belts in trains, so you might find it impossible to keep your child in their seat. A long flight for some children with ASD will not be possible if they suffer from anxiety or are unable to sit still for any length of time.

We have never flown for more than a few hours with all our boys as keeping them all occupied and sitting down and as quiet as is possible is almost impossible!

Your child may need a harness to keep them safely in their car seat, but most children will become used to car travel if they travel in a car on a regular basis. So you may be restricted to holidays that entail a car as transportation. You may also be limited by how long a journey you and they can manage. On the more positive side, you are usually in control of the environment and can bring whatever you need to keep your child occupied during the journey. Modern technology can be quite useful while travelling if your child is motivated and interested in electronic gaming devices or tablet computers.

For a plane journey, I stock up on lots of small toys or little Lego kits, which are guaranteed to keep my boys occupied for a short while.

Portable DVD players can also be very useful, not only for the journey, but also for when you arrive at your destination and do not need internet coverage to work (unlike some devices). Again, stock up on fresh (second-hand) DVDs and a few firm favourites, all of which you will probably be heartily sick of by the end of the holiday! If your child will wear head or earphones, this is a good idea as not only will it shield outside noise from your child, but it will also mean than other people do not have to listen to the film/ music. You can also buy a double headset adaptor to enable two children to watch the same film or listen to the same music. A DVD player with two mini-screens can be attached to the back of car seats for viewing.

Queuing for a plane or train may be impossible. Most travel companies will accommodate the fact that your child is unable to queue if you speak to a representative ahead of your journey and pre-arrange details. You may be offered the choice of your family getting on the transport before anyone else or even waiting until last. If you have an anxious child you may want to get on first, even if this does mean a longer time sitting and waiting to go. Your child may become anxious watching everyone else getting on and think that they are going to miss their holiday. Travel delays are not uncommon and can add additional stress and anxiety to your journey. Children with ASD tend to like to know exactly what is going to happen and at what time, so if you have outlined a time-table to them and then the timetable changes, you may have a child with meltdown to deal with.

We did not attempt to fly anywhere with our boys until they were nine years old and more able to cope with different situations. Every holiday had to be accessible by car until then. You can control your own itinerary to a certain extent by car, although unfortunately you cannot control traffic jams.

Accommodation

Your choice of accommodation needs to be considered carefully. At home, your child may sleep in their own room. While away, you will not be able to leave your child alone in a hotel bedroom. You may need to find a family room where you can all sleep together, or if you are in a hotel, as parents you may need to separate so that one of you can sleep in the same room as your child. An easier alternative may be to rent a house or cottage where you can lock the front door and know that your child is safely inside the house at night. You may need to check ahead with any holiday accommodation to see how secure it is in terms of windows and locks, and whether any outside areas are fenced or not.

If you return to the same holiday setting, then each subsequent holiday will be easier. Your child will be less anxious as they will be used to the different surroundings and know what to anticipate. If you are someone who enjoys a new experience every holiday and wishes to travel to new destinations and be adventurous, you may find it very restrictive to have to repeat the same holiday. However, if new environments are too hard to manage, then you will not enjoy your experience anyway.

We have learned that the familiar means we all get some sort of a break even if it's a case of a change more than a rest! Our boys are excited to return to somewhere they know and love rather than being anxious about somewhere they don't know. We as parents still hanker after the exotic, though, and hope that sometime in the future we will be able to be a bit more adventurous with our holidays.

Family Outings Involving Food

Some children may be on a specific diet such as a gluten-free one. They may also be very particular about what food they will eat. You may have to adapt your food cupboards and your meals to accommodate your child's diet. If your child is gluten-free, does that mean that everyone has to be gluten-free? It may be easier to cook family meals that can be adapted so that everyone eats the same thing. You may have to carry special items of food around when you go out with your family. Even if your child is not on a specific diet, they may have a self-imposed one by being very food restricted. They may only eat certain brands or makes of food or limit themselves to only a few items.

On a family picnic, I have to make six individual different sandwiches, one for each member due to each child eating only certain sandwich fillings. We unload our picnic and allocate the food. Observing this nearby, another parent opening her box of sandwiches was very surprised as she had made the same filling for everyone in her group. Basically, use whatever system best works for you.

While you may be able to accommodate your child's eating habits at home, feeding them away from the house can be problematic. Encouraging a child who is resistant to trying new foods can be stressful enough for all concerned while in the comfort of your own four walls, but attempting to encourage them eat something new in a different environment may cause a severe behavioural reaction. Always go out of the house prepared. Trying to find something suitable to eat at airports and shopping centres, in particular, can be almost impossible unless you have a small child willing to eat a very varied diet.

At one stage, I always took pizzas with me when on the rare occasions we were invited to someone's house for a meal. Firstly, the boys would be sure to eat them, and so we would avoid meltdown due to hunger or low sugar levels. Secondly, pizzas make very little mess for the host or hostess and no additional 'cooking' is required.

A packed lunch is another option. If you explain to your friends that it is not a rejection of their hospitality but that, in fact, it means you can visit them with less fuss, most people will try to understand.

All children need regular mealtimes and you may find this particularly necessary for your child with autism. If you feed your children at regular times, even if they cannot yet tell the time, their body clocks will be set to a certain time, and if food is not produced you may find your child in meltdown mode. This can be difficult to manage when travelling, being out for the day or visiting the house of a friend who does not understand the importance of your children eating on time. Always keep emergency snacks and drinks in the car or in your bag, if possible, to avoid a hungry, angry child.

Our car is always stocked with drinks and biscuits and, in fact, our youngest child treats it now as a café so as soon as we begin a journey, he asks for a juice.

What is a 'normal' family life?

Living a normal family life is not always possible. What is 'normal' anyway? The perception of family life in today's society is much changed; the old stereotype of mother, father and 2.2 children hardly exists anymore. It has been replaced by single-parent families, same-sex partnerships and unmarried parents of children. The average age at which a mother gives birth to her first child has also increased in the last generation. In the UK, with contraception readily available, people are choosing to have fewer children and sometimes choosing not to have those with known disabilities born at all. In past centuries where abortion and contraception were not readily available, people did not have the choice of whether or not to have a child, as without medical scans and tests they would have been unaware of the possibility of a child having a disability. Medical care was much less skilled, so many children would have been born without the aid of caesarean deliveries and other technical medical advances, so there were probably more disabled children born as a result. Disability may have been more common, but was it better accepted than it is now?

Only a few generations ago, special needs children were expected to be cared for in some form of institution. They were not seen out in the community and rarely lived at home with their natural parents. Children with disabilities were sent to special schools and not expected to attain much in life. There was not much therapy on offer; certainly not for children who probably had autism but were in past generations labelled as having learning disabilities and having little potential to succeed in anything. At least we have moved on from 'refrigerator mothers' and autism is now a commonly accepted diagnosis, albeit one that is often misunderstood.

So, at least now, it is 'normal' to keep your child with special needs at home with you and your family and to care for them yourself. Nobody will ask you why your child lives with you or find it strange that you look after them. There are some residential schools which, in some circumstances, may be the best option for older children who may require very specialized care and education, but young children are usually cared for in their own family settings. Unlike other disabilities that may be present at birth, autism will not become apparent for a few years at least, by which time the child is already accepted as part of his or her own family. Some parents do decide to have a baby born with a disability fostered or adopted from birth, but no parent of a child with autism would be in a position to do this as autism is not diagnosable at birth.

So, at some stage in your child's life, probably at a young age, they may be given a lifelong diagnosis of autism. How you react to this is very individual, but what you do from that time onwards will be vital for your child's future. You as a parent are the most important person in your child's life and you can make such a huge difference to how your child progresses. You will need to take on many more roles than most parents and become carer, teacher, therapist, advocate and many others. You may be required to fight battles on your child's behalf and find huge quantities of inner strength and outer energy.

Being the parent of a child with special needs can be one of the most exhausting roles you have ever had, but also one of the most rewarding as you watch your child develop skills you thought they might never acquire.

So keep going! Never give up hope! There is always light at the end of the tunnel.

USEFUL ORGANIZATIONS AND OTHER SOURCES OF INFORMATION

Autism Alliance
www.autism-alliance.org.uk
Umbrella website for 18 autism charities in the UK, giving news and information resources

Autism Independent UK
www.autismuk.com
National charity providing information about autism, including details of TEACCH

The Makaton Charity
www.makaton.org
Provides information on the use of Makaton and tutors in your area

The National Autistic Society (NAS)
www.autism.org.uk
Provides a wealth of information for parents and carers of children with autism

The National Institute for Health and Care Excellence (NICE)
www.nice.org.uk
UK Government website
Offers guidance, advice, quality standards and information services for health, public health and social care

Singing Hands
www.singinghands.co.uk
Learn how to sign for your baby or toddler

UK Government provisions for children with special needs
www.gov.uk/children-with-special-educational-needs/
extra-SEN-help
Gives details of how to request an ECHP assessment and what to do
if you disagree with a decision

USEFUL WEBSITES

www.ceacard.co.uk
For cinema cards

www.childautism.org.uk
For advice and providers of ABA programmes (formerly known as Peach)

www.treatingautism.org.uk
For advice on biomedical treatment

www.ipsea.org.uk
Independent special education advice

www.scope.org.uk
To search for grants in your area

www.autistica.org.uk
For medical research into autism

www.cerebra.org.uk
For advice including claiming DLA

www.mencap.org.uk
For support and advice, local groups and holiday activities

www.gov.uk/carers-allowance/how-to-claim

www.gov.uk/disabilty-living-allowance-children/how-to-claim

ACKNOWLEDGEMENTS

I am very grateful to the staff at Robert Hale who saw the potential in this book and took on an unpublished author, and to the staff at Crowood who saw the book through to publication.

I would like to say a big 'thank you' to my good friend Mandy Moshi, who checked the epilepsy section for me. Also to Emma Maffre who checked the EHCP section, both areas not in my expertise.

I am also hugely grateful to a new-found friend, Evie Pindsle, who has guided me through the publishing process without an agent. I owe you lunch!

There are many people who have helped us but in particular, there are some friends I wish to thank who have offered me their unfailing support for many years, often on the other end of a telephone when I was in despair and I don't know how I would have coped without them. With so much love and thanks to Sue Toombs, Mary Parr, Sally Perry and Sharon La Ronde. They are pretty awesome Godmothers too!

Over the years, we have had many wonderful ABA tutors and other carers for the boys who have made such a huge difference to our boys' lives. Some of them have become like extended family and we will always be thankful for their presence in all our lives.

But of course, the person to whom I owe the most love and thanks is my husband, Jonathan. My unfailing and uncomplaining right and left hand man. Thank you for being the best father my boys could have wished for.

INDEX